The Satan Project

BOOKS BY LON FLIPPO

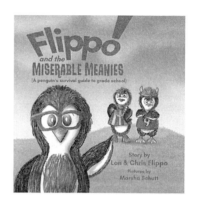

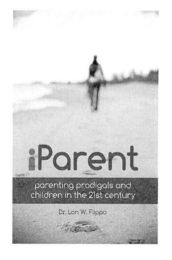

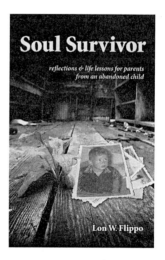

the SATAN Project

A MODERN TALE OF JOB

LON FLIPPO

iBookPublishing.com
Lenexa, Kansas

Printed in the United States of America

23 22 21 20 19   1 2 3 4 5

ISBN 978-0-9904452-7-2

Book design: Dawn M. Brandon (dawn@ravensbrook.net)

For my wife, Chris.
Because of you, the man I am is not the man I was.
Your belief in me has catapulted me to
heights I never imagined.
You are my treasure. Love you tons.

Preface

IS THE STORY OF JOB literal, or is it an allegory? Did God really set up a bet with Satan? Did Job's friends speak out of compassion, or were they just a bunch of scared cowards? No one alive can know for sure.

But what if the story was both stranger than fiction and truer than you could ever imagine?

Acknowledgments

My heart is full with the incredible support and love I have experienced on my journey. I am a lost soul without my friends and families belief in my stories.

Special love to my son, Wesley, and daughter, Ashley, for letting me "borrow" your lives in my writings.

Special thanks to (in alphabetical order—each played a significant role) Pastor Joe Anderson, Robert Curry, Kevin Ferrante, Dr. Doug Graham, President Scott Hagan, Jeff Howe, Dr. Randall Langley, Dr. Adam Sikorski, Dr. Allen Tennison, and Dr. Don Tucker.

Finally, none of this happens without the "magic" of Between the Lines with Dawn Brandon and Tammy Bicket. Honestly, none of it.

*W*hen I consider everything that exists — that every dust particle will be destroyed, that no independent existence of shape or shadow will remain — I wish death would come for me. My inner turmoil brings an insatiable thirst for death; I'm hurtling toward the annihilation we all suspect; the death of all in its wake. But then I remember that a slender flower still blossoms, extending its tendrils of undeserved love, robed in majesty, and my soul springs toward that faintest of hope.

Job

I

We are at war.

JOB
June 12, 8:06 p.m. • *Glen Ridge Forest*

AN EXPLOSION of glass and smoke assaulted my senses. I fumbled to unbuckle my seat belt and shove open the door. Agony shot through my body, and I felt myself falling. The smell of wet leaves and sodden earth assaulted my nostrils and, feeling around on all fours like a blinded animal, I scratched my hands on broken branches. My fingers quivered, and tremors shook my arms and reverberated through my body. I wretched unexpectedly, and vomit poured to the ground. Slowly stretching my back like a cat waking from a nap, the driver's side tire, which was wobbling, drew my notice.

As my head slowly cleared, I considered my surroundings with growing comprehension. Coughing to clear my congested lungs, I remembered hitting a deer. Suddenly I

3

remembered: a crazy, menacing person is trying to kill me. That's why I'm here. Should I pretend I'm dead or try to make it to the line of trees rising before me?

Panicking, I quickly scanned the area for signs of my pursuer. The forest was quiet except for a lone bird screeching and the one broken wheel on my car spinning. I felt the bird's wrath as it screamed angrily at anyone who would listen.

Teetering like a bug on a ledge, I fell to my side, desperately searching for clarity. Instead, I saw only opaque glass and dirty windows of pain and fear.

• • •

I'd started this day expecting it to be the same as yesterday. Why wouldn't I? I start every day the same. My personal likes and preferences. In fact, pity the fool who messes with my morning. Make it quiet, no waking up with "Live at 5," with those annoying smiling faces, white teeth, and perfect hair. At 5 a.m.? How is that even possible? Dark coffee and lots of caffeine have something to do with it, I'm certain. Not for me, though. I begin my day slowly. A little caffeine (double that if I slept horribly), some news and sports, toast, a hard-boiled egg, and a banana. Then I feed my dog. That's how I like it.

But today I forgot something—something of significance. I forgot about what all of us should understand with every calendar turn: Life can reach up and scratch out your eyes. It can pound you across the ears and send stars spiraling through your brain. It can grab your throat and crush the life out of you.

How tenuous life can be.

Before the day would end, back-to-back-to-back messages would announce the destruction of everything good in my life. The sheer shock, the numbness, and the emotional pain had spread over me like a desert squall. In mere moments, I'd lost everything. A hard knock on the door, the peal of the doorbell, a phone call in the middle of the night. A police officer standing on my porch.

I was unprepared. I live on the edge of certainty, but I'm never far from chaos. I can never really know what the next twenty-four hours will bring, and yet I hold out hope that every day will move through its paces and return me to the same place—safe and sound. Yet, on that day, life for me changed profoundly.

• • •

In my mind, I could still see his face. The mug of my daymare. The profile of my dreams. That incessant, smirky grin. The deep, throaty roar of laughter.

Dusk descended across the sky as the setting sun squeezed the last daylight out of the remnants of the day. Re-entering my crumpled car, I reached for my cell phone. My hands wouldn't stop trembling as I punched in my passcode and prayed for service.

"911. What's your emergency?"

"My name is Job Jenkins. I just hit a deer. I think I'm in the Glen Ridge Forest. I totaled my car. Oh . . . and someone is trying to kill me." Blinking swiftly, my vision dimmed and the ground spun . . . falling, soft leaves, broken branches . . . I blacked out.

II

Never lose sight of the fact that
our enemy hunts us,
plotting murder in the first degree.

June 12, 8:17 p.m.

WAKING IN AN AMBULANCE will pretzel the strongest mind. Shades of gray metal lined a tomb full of tubes, machines, and talking bodies. "What's your name?" A smiling face appeared dimly in my vision. "Huh?" Gathering my wits, I asked the most ignorant of all questions — a question already asked and answered: "Where am I?"

"You're in an ambulance on your way to County Medical. Now, tell us your name!"

"My name is Job." A deer floating across my hood, a wobbling wheel, and a smug, malevolent face flitted across my mind. Blackness slowly threatened to overtake my mind. Fighting to stay conscious, I opened my mouth and screamed the words:

"Someone is trying to murder me."

Blinking fast, I tried to push back the creeping darkness. "What did he say?"

"I have no idea."

County Medical Hospital, 9:29 p.m.

Pale, gray shadows settled over the room. A solitary light glowed faintly under a wooden shelf. My wife Joy, sleeping awkwardly in a sterile hospital chair, murmured quietly. I stayed silent. My head pulsed with a dull ache, but I remained vigilant. How did I get here? Was I dreaming, or just plain *One Flew Over the Cuckoo's Nest* nuts? Relaxing slightly, I peered into the dark room, attempting to make sense of my situation.

My life is a story. I imagined it in a particular way—a rousing introduction, interesting characters, perplexing drama, twists and turns, all followed by a dramatic conclusion chock full of glory and love. But it hasn't happened that way. And you know why? Because I forgot about the villains. Or in this case, the one bad dude. There seemed to be only one way for my story to end, and it wasn't anything like I'd imagined.

The curtain rises on this whodunit mystery play. The actor maintains a silent vigil on a blackened stage devoid of props and scenery. My personal drama plays in high definition on an earthly landscape, and I am mesmerized, like a bystander watching death explode in living color.

Back to the beginning. Back to a moment before I even had a clue someone knew my name and was determined to destroy me. And when I say destroy, I mean total, utter destruction of everything I know and hold sacred. Like a delicate jellyfish, I wash briefly onto a sandy beach, one moment full of life, the next simply vanishing with the receding tide.

All I can hope to do is survive. Honestly, that's the best I've got. Survive. Chaos is erupting in my family.

Self-pity vanished in a microsecond as the weight of that thought stunned me back to real life. My family!

"Joy?" Turning my head, I said it louder, "Joy!"

"You're awake. Thank God."

"Babe, are the kids safe?"

"Are *you* okay?"

Joy stood quickly. Gripping my hand, she whispered, "Don't worry about us; this is about you."

"You don't understand, Joy. We're all in trouble. Call the cops now!"

"Job, relax!"

"No!" Raising my head, I started screaming. "He's going to kill us. He's going to kill us!" Seeing no understanding in my wife's face, I once again screeched, "He's going to kill us!"

"Who, honey? Who is trying to kill us?"

"Abaddon." I regained control of my body and mind, and then spoke again, quietly but firmly. "His name is Abaddon."

"What the . . . " The pinch was sharp, the needle long.

"That should help, Mrs. Jenkins. He'll be out for a few hours."

Lowering my head, my tongue thick and dry, I heard the words in my head, but my voice was silent. "His name is Abaddon."

*All of us are destined to face an
ultimate test of our faith.*

ABADDON
June 10, 9:13 a.m. • *Gloucester Business Park*

THIS TEST OF JOB was my chance to prove Elohim wrong. What would be my best prospect for sabotaging Job? The threat of death, of course. All humans instinctively fear death and would do almost anything to avoid facing it. I'd been watching this fool for several weeks, and I was so sick of his pathetic rosy, one-sided view of Elohim. "Elohim loves me. Elohim is awesome." Blah, blah, blah! What was it Job once said to his friends at the local pool hall? "Even though he spills my guts on the ground, I will still place my trust in him"? Yeah, that was it. Job, the eternal optimist. Here's the problem with that way of thinking. The optimist takes credit for the positives in his life and plays down his own responsibility for the negative.

15

Now, maybe that was an angle worth considering. I could narrow his options, distort the evidence, shift the responsibility, and Job just might curse Elohim for his pain and suffering. That could work! Push Job to lose hope. Loss of hope leads to blaming. Blame gives birth to fear. Fear quickens death. It really is quite simple: blame anything or anyone. Blame your spouse. Your culture. Eventually, like everyone before him, Job would blame Elohim.

Hatred of this man with his sickeningly pure faith and trust in my mortal enemy surged into an uncontrollable rage. "Job Jenkins must die!" I screamed. Spittle flew from my mouth, spraying my wide-eyed, fearful herd of demon associates. Aimlessly wandering the floor, waiting for instructions, they tromped around the grubby warehouse buried deep in a forgotten business park. Here, it was easy to blend into the wasteland of humanity, but my patience was wearing thin. Lumps of clay, these fragile humans moaned, griped, and murmured about the taste of morning coffee, spam email, and the ever-changing weather. Distasteful as I found it, blending in was a necessary challenge if I were to maneuver closer to my selected target, this distasteful, irksome human, Job Jenkins.

Glancing at my horde of followers, I fought conflicting urges to shake my head and laugh out loud. Snorting ridiculously through their noses, their pathetic expressions were more goofy grins than sinister sneers. Rather than a capable, competent cohort I could depend on, they reminded me of a herd of bison racing mindlessly over a cliff to their deaths. Was there no one I could rely on besides myself? Must I always save the day? Couldn't anybody, somebody, just once, take the initiative and make a decision without second-guessing what color of underwear to put on that day?

I swallowed the anger that rose within me until my throat hurt, and I could no longer restrain it—anger at Elohim, disgust with my miserable cronies, hatred for this man Job. "I don't care what Elohim said," I thundered. "Hear my words: Job will die. I don't mean metaphysical, emotional or spiritual death. I'm talking blood-drenched, gut-spilling, brain-dead, heart-stopping, physical death. I want him dead: D-E-A-D." I paused dramatically, then continued, "But—he's mine!" My eyes scanned the room, searching out any twinge of reluctance, an ounce of denial, one tiny hint of betrayal.

My front pocket buzzed. I hate these stupid contraptions. Why did we use these inefficient human devices when we are transcendent beings? Criminy! Just send me a mind message. Small-minded humans believe that a handheld device validates their personal existence. They believe that, somehow, they are worthwhile because they own the latest piece of plastic, wire, and silicon? I chortled out loud, realizing that another of my ruses was working. Humans were swallowing the lie I'd been telling them about what gives their lives value—hook, line, and sinker!

Pulling the annoying device from my pocket, I moved outside to avoid having to look at the moronic faces surrounding me, begging for direction. "What do we do next, boss?" Pathetic, whiny, worthless wastes of time and space. They disgusted me.

The text read simply, "Thou art summoned." Seriously, who in the universe talks like that? Elohim's pathetic, pure little doves too often messed with my mind—bruising my psyche, pushing my buttons. Still, they feared me. And who could blame them? For I was a formidable foe. Banished from the heavens, I had laid claim to terra firma, where I patrolled the plains, made the mountains my own, and possessed the beaches. Everything was my domain. Prince of the Air. The Dark One. Ruler of planet Earth. That was me.

Yet when Elohim beckoned, He expected me to drop everything like a good little pup and run to my master with tail-waging, slobbering glee? Dream on, jokers.

I laughed loudly, and my mind switched from jokers to Batman. Quickly, I texted, "Same bat time, same bat channel?"

Grinning like the proverbial Cheshire cat, I pulled two of the five sticks of gum from the pack. Sour strawberry—such irony; something so sweet yet so sour. Sorta like me? Chuckling again, I folded the gum in half, rolled up the pieces, and popped them into my mouth.

"What losers," I said out loud as I waited for the response. My thoughts deserved to be heard by someone, so I just tossed them out there. No caution, just in-your-face, crushing disdain. Deal with it!

There it was. The reply: "Yes. In 1 hour."

So, it was on. Abaddon versus the cronies. Me versus the Grand Poobah. The young punk battling the hosts of obedient angelic robots. I couldn't wait. Pressing my fingers across the buttons with more force than necessary, I texted my daring response.

"Prepare to be boarded." Two could play this game. Excited rage fluttered through my brain like agitated bats. "I'm coming," I roared, shouting to the sky. Then, breathing deeply, I quietly whispered to myself: "I'm coming."

One hour later • Heavenly Council

Lord of the Cherubim . . . Prince of the Air . . . Lucifer. Some call me Beelzebub, Belial, Apollyon, the Great Dragon, the Red Serpent, or the Devil. I prefer Abaddon. Originating from an ancient Hebrew dialect, it means Destroyer. Has a nice ring, don't you think? Abaddon, the Destroyer. Maybe? Maybe not. Think of me what you will.

Still, I like it when people underestimate me or assume they understand my essence, thinking I'm some dreamy television star with flowing locks and daggers for eyes. Modern media has made my world and power seem approachable. Push a button, flick a switch, and presto, I appear. Say the magic word—Legion, Freak, or Superstar—and I become palpable, innocuous—maybe even lovable?

Keep thinking you know me—red cape, horns, pitchfork, and tail—demon, gargoyle, roaring lion, or mysterious alien organism. Or better yet, keep pretending I don't exist. That way you won't notice when I creep from the shadows, ready, waiting, and eager to slash your throat. Whether you don't believe in me or believe in the caricature, you'll pay either way. I'm mayhem.

The summons from Elohim was burned into my mind like a maddening mathematical equation. Bits of code swirled and floated, cascading slowly into an aggravating demand, not a request. Materializing like Captain Kirk from *Star Trek* wasn't just cool, it was plain awesome. Arriving late, I strolled into the meeting and stood quietly in the back row. Forming a half circle, those in attendance stood silently in a white spot in which light spilled in a perfect circle surrounding each being. Alone, I stood in darkness. I looked at the weird, sickly glow that lighted the faces of those in attendance. Completely visible, they appeared neither holographic nor solid in form. It still amazed me how Elohim allowed us to be both in spirit and body simultaneously.

Elohim was speaking. "The Tree of the Knowledge of Good and Evil was never about the restriction. The restriction was the gift. I never kept them from knowing good. The restriction only kept them from knowing and experiencing evil. What is best for mankind? To become like one of us? Capable of knowing everything?" Is it to reach out and take fruit from the Tree of Life? To eat and live forever? Or would that only have allowed them to live forever in their miserable and fallen state, eternally separated from fellowship with me?

His statement offered so many possibilities. "Eat and you will die?" Wrong! It never has been about good versus evil. It's always been about knowledge. What you know. Who you might become. Doing rather than becoming. Making your own choices. Gain knowledge or die.

An intriguing idea started coalescing in my mind. That's it, I decided.

Stepping forward, I voiced my challenge, "What if you stir humans' resentment of your restrictions and diminish their value as a gift? Would that make them more likely to rebel? Or skew the over-under?" From firsthand experience, I knew that when you distance yourself from Elohim's will, you create a chasm between you and him. For that reason, I decided to focus my attention on urging humans to desire what God had forbidden, knowing that they would reach for it every time. What better way was there to separate God's creation from the love and protection of their Creator?

Suddenly, I was no longer in darkness; a spotlight of white-hot light streamed from the ceiling and focused on me, causing a small trickle of sweat to run from my armpit down my side. After a moment of scrutiny, during which I stood silently, the light clicked off, and I was once more in darkness. Fine, don't acknowledge my presence at the council. I like the dark. I relaxed, allowing the blackness to envelop me and fill my heart.

IV

Be well balanced and always alert,
because your enemy, the devil,
roams around incessantly, like a
roaring lion looking for its prey to devour.

1 PETER 5:8 TPT

JOB
June 12, 9:54 a.m. • *Lima Joe's Coffee Shop*

BEFORE EVERYTHING CHANGED on that fateful day, blissfully
ignorant, I half-stumbled into my familiar java hut, Lima Joe's,
for my mid-morning latte. Glancing around, I spotted the usual
local faces: Eddie, the realtor, always scanning the multiple
listing service, praying for a hot new listing; a couple of financial investors in their suits; an elderly couple behind the USA
Today sports section and a series of scattered sudokus. Throw
in a couple of young adults, faces buried in their devices, and
a befuddled mother yammering away on her cell phone, and
you had the usual crowd. Strangers got the evil eye if they even
glanced at a seat within six feet of someone's private domain.

In the sea of familiar faces, I saw him — an unknown, a
mystery man, a complete stranger. Walking up to me boldly,

he pushed his perfect face in my space, laughed, and said three little words: "Welcome to hell."

I won't forget that face. I never will. A clean shave. Blazing black hair, dark eyebrows, and those creepy, piercing, glinting pupils. Staring. Never blinking, green and black orbs. They locked with my eyes and seemed to penetrate to the core of my being.

He proceeded to tell me—very matter-of-factly—that he was going to screw with my health, mess with my family, and take everything I owned. Pausing, as if he anticipated my shocked disbelief, he added softly, "You have been weighed in the balance and found wanting." Turning, he started to walk away, then paused; he turned back and got in my face once more, adding, "My name is Abaddon."

"Huh? Do I know you? What's your problem?" Stunned, my ego bruised, and more than a little fear growing at the edges of my subconscious, I fumbled for a snappy retort: "Hey, ya filthy animal. Kiss my keister!"

Smiling, he casually walked away as if nothing had transpired. But something had, and, helplessly, I felt that my day—maybe my life—had been changed dramatically . . . irredeemably . . . against the mundane backdrop of Lima Coffee. I glanced around, looking for someone to acknowledge the conversation I'd just had with this nutso creature who had invaded my world unbidden. Tiny, bright screens illuminated haggard faces. Zero eye contact. It was as if it had never happened. My mind felt mushy with the insanity of it all. This Abaddon is insane.

Or is he? What if I'm the one who is insane? Had I only imagined the entire conversation?

Tuesday-morning coffee lay busted like a mug and saucer that had slipped to the floor. Thinking about what had just happened was making my stomach do flip-flops. A freak walks up, threatens me, laughs, and walks away. It was one surprise I never would have dreamed of.

Holding my cup high, I let the hot steam from my latte radiate upward to warm my face. I was still in shock when, as if messing with my mind wasn't enough, Abaddon returned with such precision of purpose that I did not have time to react. I never saw it coming. A flash of black hair, a leering face spinning to grin at me. A touch of the hand, a light brushing of air, hushed words, "Let me show you," and instantly, I was spinning through a vortex of color and sound.

Flicked like a flea from the coffee shop into a Matrix-style time machine, the unnatural change in scenery overwhelmed my senses. Before I could regain my composure, the coffee shop with its rich blue curtains and craftsman-style oak counters had simply vanished.

In that moment, Earth was a distraction that stole precious minutes from time. Time is limited. I understood the concept. My body was not asleep, nor was I dreaming. A simple touch, and I was instantly transported from my present reality to a place I did not know. Later, I would come to understand. The inner door to heaven only coincides with the outer door to Earth at carefully arranged moments. I did not possess the skill to orchestrate the obscure computations required to predict the time for safe passage. That was reserved for those from a higher dimension. It was a marvelous system that prevented the deepest, most sacred of secrets from escaping. The coffee shop seemed exactly as before, but my body floated as if detached. Where was I? Why was I here?

Like a shimmering horizon coming into view, this new dimension came into focus. Glancing upward, I saw a metallic-looking lid with no handles. I was in a clear, color-less tube. Stomping, I felt a solid surface beneath my feet but sensed no depth. Pressing my hand against the side of my prison, my fingers disappeared into a swirling mist. The mist enveloped me from top to bottom and on every side. Strange, it covered me, yet I could see beyond it—beyond the tube. Weak from fright, I tried desperately to summon new strength from deep within. I pressed forward but was stopped about a foot inside. My hands and feet could pass through the mist, but I could not move beyond the barrier. Outside my cocoon, people were walking by as if I didn't exist. I screamed wildly for help, but the futility of my efforts quickly overwhelmed me, and I slowly slid to the floor. Rubbing my hands gently over the surface below me, I found it surprisingly warm to the touch and smooth. My head rested against mist swirling around me, and it felt good, comfortable. I relaxed slightly, accepting my fate, and let my mind replay the events of that crazy morning.

There had been about three or four "before" and "after" moments in my life—when something happens that splits reality into two pieces. There's a clear "before" and a definite "after." In each of those moments, a clear choice lay before me, to view what was transpiring as something good or some-thing evil. Was this one such split? Was this my moment?

Gone was the sweet smell of glories past. The term of my joy-filled life had expired. I inhaled and felt the sting of a new reality.

V

Commitment to Elohim does not exempt us
from heartbreak, frustration, or pain,
but through pain and suffering,
we enter into the kingdom of Elohim,
where we gain wisdom.

JOB
June 12 • *Heavenly Council*

SEVERAL HOURS HAD PASSED, although I had no real concept of passing time. Sitting quietly in my translucent tube, I grew weary of yelling, pondering, and watching angelic beings, or whatever they were, go about their business completely oblivious to my plight.

Funny, you remember the strangest things in the weirdest moments. Clever quips from my dad floated through my mind. "The beginning holds the end," he had once said. My father, Wesley, a professor for many years and revered by his students for his straightforward, truthful sayings, used to say, "If you want to meet good people, go to good places."

"Church," my dad had added, "that's the best place to meet good people. They're not all good people, but sinners looking for salvation are better than saints looking for sin." Tears welled in my eyes as I remembered my father. I'd give anything right now to see him standing over a stove, handing out truth that sizzled like bacon in an open frying pan.

Let me take you one step back to where it started.

Her name was Joy, and when she walked into the church potluck that night, she brought "Joy" physically and emotionally and dumped it on me like a bucket of cold water on a scorching hot day. Four kids, two dogs, and thirty-four years later, we had a good life—brick-and-mortar two-story house complete with a double garage, granite counter tops, rainfall showers, hardwood floors, a redwood deck, shrubs, and a sprinkler system. The kids were healthy—full of spirit and moxie. They weren't perfect, but who is?

There was love—lots and lots of love. Joy lived up to her name and showered me—lathered me—with joy. Suddenly, in spite of my heavenly surroundings, a sense of fear and dread gripped my heart. What if everything Abaddon had told me was true? Was it really possible that I was about to lose everything?

JOB
June 13, 11:34 a.m. • *Windermere Financial Services*

Funny, life can fall to pieces in a matter of hours.

The pattern seemed obscure in real time; later, it crystallized perfectly. Three calls, three dramatic events, three consecutive days.

"Mr. Jenkins."

"Yes, Caleb." Tucked inside my comfy office, my personal assistant was calling my desk phone. Why do we even have desk phones? I wondered.

"A Mrs. Harvey from Morgan Hill Academy is on line 3. Some type of emergency."

My kids' school principal. I impatiently waited for the click that signaled that Caleb had switched me to the other line and quickly said, "This is Job Jenkins. Are my kids okay?"

"I'm sorry to disturb you at work, but we can't reach your wife, and I didn't want to wait any longer to contact you."

Joy's silence troubled me, but I pushed it to the back of my mind as new fears arose for my children. "What's wrong?"

"It's your children, John and Janise. They came to the nurse's station feeling sick and complaining of headaches. Before we could figure out what was happening, they both passed out. We're rushing them to Cox Medical Center in San Jose. Again, I'm so sorry."

I dropped the phone, my mind wondering where my wife was. Grabbing my cell phone, wallet, and keys, I shouted at Caleb, "Walk with me to the car. I've got an emergency." Slamming the car door shut, I dialed Joy's cell phone. When it was sent to voice mail after the first ring, I knew her phone was off. At the gym? Morning nap? I left a hasty voice mail asking her to meet me at the hospital, then tapped out a quick text, lurched into reverse, and tore through the parking lot. The look of fear on Caleb's face as I screeched my tires and raced away was alarming. Glancing in the rearview mirror, I understood his fear. A crazed face glared back at me.

. . .

After consulting with puzzled doctors who could offer me no satisfactory answers, I felt totally alone with my fears. Inside that hospital room alone with my pale and silent children, a hush of terror fell over me. I brushed the hair from my daughter's forehead and felt a tear roll down my cheek and splash onto the pillow beside her head. Glancing over at my son and seeing tubes sticking out of his nose, I felt my knees buckle. I broke and fell to my knees between my children's beds. All pretenses gone, I wept hard. Drawing unexpected strength from a nurse's hand on my shoulder, I clawed my way back to a standing position. My brain searched for clarity as I cleared my nose and wiped my eyes. What was wrong with my kids? Where was my wife?

VI

Why doesn't Elohim correct what could be undone in the blink of an eye?

JOB
June 14, 11:57 p.m. • *Home, 1457 Trillium Court*

IN MY CLOSET is an outlet neatly tucked beside the man-chest where I place my ring, wallet, and phone. Every night, I plug in my phone amongst the shirts, skirts, and shoes. Like most people, we'd ditched our landline. If you want to reach me past 11 p.m., sorry. I'll get your message at 6 a.m. when I awake. Tonight felt different. In anxiety over my kids laying helpless in a nearby hospital, I cradled my phone. Hoping against hope, I prayed it wouldn't ring.

My legs felt stiff. My car accident had left me feeling like I'd lost a boxing match—a brutal workout for a man in his mid-fifties. I was just thankful Joy's fender bender hadn't been much more than an inconvenience. What were the odds of us both having accidents within 24 hours? Ordinarily I'd say it was an incredible coincidence. But there was nothing ordinary about this.

Lying in bed felt good, but sleep was still hours away. A notification blinked on my screen; strange, I didn't hear the phone ring. Tapping it, I saw that a message was waiting. "Urgent . . . Please call us ASAP . . . thank you . . . Pacific Beach California Police."

My stomach dropped. Pacific Beach is where my oldest son lives. My fingers trembled as I once again read the message, then highlighted the number and pressed. Simultaneously, I walked to the edge of the bed, where my wife was sleeping in spite of her minor accident earlier that day. A few bumps and bruises, and yet somehow she was sleeping soundly while I prowled like a restless cat. Yet, I was thankful for her presence, so thankful. I gently shook her shoulder. Rolling over, she groggily looked at me, fear growing in her eyes. I whispered, "James."

A brief silence passed, and then I heard the phone ringing. Pushing the speaker button, I waited. "Pacific Beach Police, how may I assist you?"

"Yes. I received a text message asking me to call." Swallowing hard, I felt the dryness of my raspy throat.

"Name?"

"Excuse me?"

"Your name."

"Oh. Sorry. Job Jenkins."

"Give me a second."

"Huh?"

"I said, give me a moment to check the details."

Silently, I waited, my mind dull, my heart beating swiftly.

"Okay. Sorry. I need you to talk with Sargent Weatherly."

"Uh, why?"

"Sargent Weatherly will explain everything. I'll transfer you to his desk."

What the heck? This was hell racing to my front door. I looked at my wife. She was snow-blanket white and staring blankly at me. Instantly I began pacing the room. Diverting my eyes, I stared at the wall, looking for an escape from this perilous spot.

"Is this Mr. Job Jenkins?"

"Yes."

"My name is Sargent Francis Weatherly, and I have bad news regarding your son James."

A low, guttural moan slid across the room from my wife's lips.

"Hello? Are you there?"

"Yes. Is our son alive?"

"Truthfully, we don't know. Eyewitnesses are reporting his apparent abduction from Mission Street here in Pacific Beach. It appears your son was kidnapped at approximately 12:38 a.m. this morning."

"Sir? Are you there?"

"Yes. I'm sorry, we're kinda in shock here."

"I understand, Mr. Jenkins. Are you able to get on a plane and come out here? We have some important questions and need your help."

"Yes. Of course."

"I'm sorry Mr. Jenkins, this has to be tough."

Silence gripped the air, and I wondered if we'd been disconnected.

"Thanks for holding, Mr. Jenkins. If you have a pen, I'll give you the information to contact me upon your arrival. We'll have a police car waiting for you at the airport."

I dropped my phone and held my crying wife. No words were uttered as we let the waves of panic roll over our hearts. Tears streaming down my face, I heard my wife's sobbing as I hold her throbbing body. Then I stopped, listening intently. There. I heard something. I'm positive. Amidst the cries of a broken mother and the sobs of a troubled father, I heard a chuckle of laughter. A distinct, guttural laugh. Laughter from the throat of Abaddon. The same pile of poppycock from Lima Joe's. He's behind my son's abduction. He's behind my kids' sickness . . . I just knew it! What's next? This much I knew, Abaddon was real. He wanted to kill me and my family.

I quickly showered, shaved, and dressed. I noticed the clock: 1:27 a.m. I wondered how long I had to get to the airport before the flight Joy was booking. Glancing into the misty mirror, I wiped away the steam, when I heard my phone chirping. Wiping my face and hands, I picked up the phone. Glancing down, I saw that I had fourteen new emails and eight texts, moments after I had just cleared my accounts. What in the world?

Before my eyes lay a sea of alerts and transactions denied, accounts frozen, and other general financial mayhem. Hours later I would learn that my accounts had all been frozen, and massive charges were being levied against my financial portfolios. Bottom line, my advisor said, "Your identity has been stolen, and until this is cleared up, everything is frozen."

Standing in a steamy bathroom with a loosely tucked towel, I gazed into the mirror. Suddenly I felt like a lost, confused fifteen-year-old. The sound of the door opening yanked me from my self-loathing; Joy entered the room, but she looked anything but joyful. Anger pulled her mouth taught—that sweet mouth—and angst flowed from her lips.

"Job, what's going on? I'm trying to buy your airline tickets, but all our cards have been denied."

Perfect. "I'm sorry babe. I'll fix this."

"You'd better." She sounded close to breaking, and it scared me. "I can't deal with one. More. Problem," she said emphatically. Then, choking on tears, she fled the bathroom, sobbing.

Yeah, me either. "I'm sorry," I call after her. "Don't worry, I've got cash." But it isn't enough. What next?

June 15, 9:37 a.m. • *San Diego International Airport*
Visiting San Diego is an easy jump. There are cheap direct flights, and the pull of seeing the ocean and family is strong. Our oldest son lives there, and it's arguably one of the most beautiful places in the United States. Today, my usual euphoria was replaced by dread. My head throbbed, my stomach flip-flopped with anxiety, and the man sitting next to me stank of dirty clothes, body odor, and sour breath. I pushed to get off the plane as soon as it landed. Scurrying to the bathroom, I relieved myself and splashed water on my face. I wished Joy were with me, but our sick kids needed her home.

VII

We either believe that Elohim fights for us
or that he's letting Abaddon destroy us.

JOB
June 12 • *Heavenly Council*

MY EYES SLOWLY ADJUSTED to the dim light emitted by hundreds of gleaming consoles. Desperate to understand where I was, I focused on the screens hovering in space, conveying imagery from what looked like Earth.

"So," I said out loud, "Elohim is watching?" Shaking off the images cascading through my mind, I focused my thoughts on my present situation.

From my mist-filled prison, I could tell that something important was happening. Hundreds of angels and cherubim filled a giant room. My tube-shaped cage was in a corner in the back of the room. I felt invisible, like Casper the ghost, yet strangely, I could hear and see everything. Nobody noticed my existence, no matter whether I shouted, cried, or sulked.

It began simple and pure. A pristine gathering of those who worshiped him. Elohim was summoning the angels, cherubs, and archangels to the heavenly council. Seconds before the opening refrain, Abaddon strode into the high council with the smugness of a cocky, know-it-all jackhole.

From my translucent tube of swirling mist, I had a front-row seat.

"Well, hey!" he laughingly smirked. "If it isn't Elohim's pretty little choir kids." A husky, strong-jawed captain named Topek quickly moved toward Abaddon with his fists balled and teeth clenched.

"Bring it on, big boy," Abaddon beckoned, his arm gesturing slowly around the room. "People want to taste blood."

"Don't do it Topek," whispered an angel.

"He's not worth it," chimed in a seraph.

"Actually. I *am* worth it," Abaddon said, snapping off each word crisp and clear. His piercing, green eyes glistened as a sparkle of rage flashed in his pupils.

Topek's tightened mouth relaxed, and releasing his fists, he moved carefully to his left, to a prescribed place between himself and this self-professed Prince of the Air. My eyes widened as I saw how Abaddon made his presence known to those near him. In that moment, I knew. I understood why legions both followed and cowered before the powerful rage of this complex and mysterious being. It all made sense. Abaddon was a force of power in both my world *and* his, a presence I would never comprehend. Sauntering coolly down the aisle, he paused briefly, his gaze flickering upward. Fascinated, my own gaze lengthened, and I understood Abaddon's hesitation.

No sound escaped Elohim's throat; there was only a slight movement of his fingers as Elohim motioned for Abaddon to approach him.

Elohim sat within the blackest, deepest mass of leather and metal my eyes had ever seen. The captains of his guard stood silently, like stone sentries. I saw no fear in their posture or expression, only peaceful repose. Abaddon fidgeted slightly, like a nervous child before the school principal, waiting for Elohim to speak. The world split before me. Fear and rage fumed on one side, peace and hope flourished on the other. Suddenly Abaddon no longer held my attention. The raw power of Elohim restored my senses. I did not understand what was happening, but I didn't care. "Magnificent," I mumbled to myself. "Absolutely mind-blowing. Beyond brilliant!"

The air stilled, and the room hushed in reverent silence. Feeling my breathing slow and my pulse relax, I thought, Who can tame the heart of a demon? What can cut hatred from the fabric of a heart and raise a banner of hope? "Elohim," I whispered. "Elohim."

For a fraction of a second, I was sure he had heard me, for as I said it, I could have sworn that he looked in my direction. But his attention was on my tormentor. "Where have you been?" Elohim demanded of him. Crafting his words carefully, he did not honor Abaddon by using his name, instead, only acknowledging his presence. "Testing the edges of light? Challenging the depths of darkness?"

"Just here and there." Abaddon quietly pronounced the words. "You know, just traveling the void, searching for darkness."

"Did you by chance happen to notice my servant Job?"

I felt the blood drain from my face, and my chest tightened. Had Elohim just said my name?

I've been here before. Walking up on a group of people, I feel the climate change without a whisper of wind. Without saying a word, the voices hush or trail away. Like a diver fighting his way to the water's surface, starving for air, I know the truth. Deep down inside, I know the subject of the chatter. This is about me. I listen quietly as the pretense of talk about the weather or the local sports team follows its course. Nodding my head, grinning slightly, I scheme a clever retort that drops them in their tracks and shuts their duplicitous traps. Maybe, in an insane moment, I scream obscenities to shell-shocked eyes. Maybe, even worse, I unleash unchecked violence upon noses and mouths. Instead, I swallow hard, glance at the floor, and say, "Good talk. Sorry, I need to get back to work." In a moment, it's over. I cringe; someone else smirks.

My heart stopped when I heard Elohim say, "Did you by chance happen to notice my servant Job?"

"Actually, I did." Abaddon paused dramatically, as if he expected Elohim to say something else. Hearing nothing, he continued. I noticed the hard swallow in his throat before he spoke again.

"Job's not an idiot." Elohim didn't flinch, so Abaddon pressed forward. "Do you honestly think he fears you just because he loves you? Nobody has it better than Job! He's a spoiled rotten kid. Everything's handed to him on a silver platter. You've given him the finest blessings on the planet. Possessions, riches, safety, family—you snap your fingers, and *poof...*" Abaddon snapped his fingers, punctuating the statement; "...he has it." The snap reverberated through the silent council.

Abaddon paused to catch his breath, then continued his tirade. Smiling slightly, he snarled sarcastically, shifted gears, and without warning began strangely speaking in old English. The guttural tone of and hate-filled words clashed discordantly with the high-mannered speech, eliciting squirms and twitches from those who listened. "O, thou grand writers of the universe's destiny. What if thou didst forswear Job, smiting him in the entrails, oft besmirching him with troubles and turmoil? What if thou didst reach down and snatch away all his trinkets, toys, and tots? Might not hot, angry, filthy curse words speweth from his mouth?"

Suddenly I realized I wasn't breathing. In fact, I was holding my breath. I couldn't feel my pulse. Was my heart still beating? My body was in a state of shock, and my mind felt dead. Images froze, and time ceased to exist as Elohim, in a tone low and soft, said the words I never expected and would never forget.

"Fine."

Fine? Panic started to overwhelm me. *Fine?!?*

"Go ahead—do what you want with him." He paused, and for a brief moment I thought I heard sadness. But my attention turned quickly from him to me by Elohim's next words. "Test him, take away his possessions. Vex him physically. *But...*" pausing, he pointed his finger at Abaddon; "...don't, and I mean this, don't murder him." Elohim's eyes bored into Abaddon's for a brief but poignant moment. "Now go!"

What? What did I do to deserve this? Why me?

Abaddon awkwardly bowed and shuffled backward. Turning around slowly, he walked carefully toward the open door at the back of the heavenly council. With each step, his confidence seemed renewed, and he soon was striding gracefully, with renewed arrogance. As he passed Topek and the other angels, he turned his head slightly and grinned.

June 15, 9:42 a.m.

The smell of fresh urine wafted to my nostrils. Glancing around, wide-eyed, instead of seeing Elohim's throne room, I found myself staring into a water-spotted mirror in a men's restroom in San Diego International Airport. Gazing intently into the mirror, I peered at my own face, which stared back at me, flushed with shock and disbelief.

In my peripheral vision, I caught a blur of fast movement. Suddenly, Abaddon was staring back at me over my shoulder. Leaning forward, he whispered in my ear. "Job, I don't give a rat's rear end what Elohim said. I'm going to rip out your entrails, wrap them around your neck, and watch you die." Without a second breath, he emphasized his last word. "Literally."

Turning his head slightly, he looked directly into the mirror, met my eyes wide with horror, grinned, and walked away.

"You okay, bro?" The stranger standing next to me at the sink looked concerned. Shaking my head as if to clear the cobwebs, I mumbled, "Yeah. Sorry. Just tired, I guess."

"I hear you man. Travel sucks!"

"So does life." I fumbled with my backpack, then scurried for the exit like a scared rabbit running from a crazed wolf. Zigging and zagging, I fought my way to ground transportation, praying for Elohim to spare me. Suddenly the thought seized me—what about my family? Guilt washed over me, and a tear slipped from my red, irritated eyes. Let me *die*, if I must, but please spare my family.

Ahead, I saw a police officer holding a sign with my name scrawled in black letters. "Spare my family," I fervently threw the prayer to the sky, "Spare my son."

"Hi. Job Jenkins?"

The police officer's greeting snapped me back to reality. "Uh . . . Yes," I responded, obviously not sounding too convincing.

"Can I see some identification?"

Setting my bag down, I fumbled for my wallet.

"Are you sick?" the officer asked gently, sizing me up with a critical eye.

"Uh. No. But, I, don't feel so good."

"Thought so. You look white as a ghost. Sargent Weatherly is at the station. Let's go."

Ghost, I thought. If only . . . I was pretty sure I'd just seen one evil whack job.

VIII

*He was a murderer from the beginning
and a hater of truth.*

JOHN 8:43–44 TLB

ABADDON
June 12 • Heavenly Council

THE UNIVERSE WAS CRUMPLING like a thin piece of paper before my eyes. Like a black hole spiraling to infinity, everything I thought I knew was disappearing before my eyes.

An open smirk was dangerous in front of Elohim, but the thought twirled through my rage, This will end badly for Job. Very badly. Bowing slightly, I spun on my heels and strode quickly up the walkway toward the exit. My fine leather shoes clapped on the dark-stained flooring. The sound invigorated my sense of power. "Very badly Elohim," I muttered to the back wall.

Elohim's voice pierced me, buckling my knees. Pain exploded in my ears, and I struggled to breathe as his voice thundered from the front of the room. "You may understand reality, Abaddon. No one is your equal in studying the past, but you need to understand the future. Heed my words. Job will not die."

Why did Elohim continue to bully me and deny me my prize? Why did he play with my psyche? My emotions? My pride? Wasn't it enough that he had cast me out of the heavens? Why the constant humiliation? He had disregarded me, misunderstood me, but I would never let him forget me. I would pursue my plan regardless of Elohim's command. No person, place, or thing—no God—would order my life. The only supreme being who could command my attention was me. I dictate terms for the rest of the human race, and Job would be no different. He would fall victim to my plan for all of them.

Anger contorted my face and spread to my fists. Balling them tightly, I felt the juice once again flowing through my bloodstream. I would not argue with Elohim, but I would not obey. My only response would be murder. Job's murder, exacting and mercilessly executed.

With measured steps, I strode to the door. I would not let them see me tremble. I exited the room, rounded the corner, and leaned against a smooth stone slab of a wall. Feeling the cold surface pushed my rage to the edge. Smashing my palms flat against the cold stone, I screamed into the night. Deep, primal shrieks tore from my throat. "Damn them. Damn them all!"

• • •

ABADDON
Years earlier • Kingdom of Heaven

Roaming the world, helping lost fools and ignorant doofs might sound exciting to the average angelic being. For me, it was comparable to rubbing superglue between my fingers and sticking them to my nose. Bored out of my brain, I went out for a stroll and soon found myself walking up a local trail to the top of a nearby mountain. Morning was breaking. I stared silently at the horizon, barely able to breathe. Not from exhaustion or the breathtaking view of twin lakes ringed by trees and valleys. No. It was far more complex than simply needing extra cardio time in the gym. The day before had been a day I would never forget.

I had awakened in a heated sweat, my skin boiling. My existence was choking the life out of me. One single, solitary thought obsessed me. A fluttering flame spitting against an icy blast. The thought lingered: What if?

Sputtering, it resolutely marched forward, consuming every fiber and sinew of my being. Like warm massage oil, it trickled through the hairs of my arms. I sensed the blood pumping through my veins, but it felt new, raw, more powerful. Seconds later, something started worming its way deeper into my bloodstream. The hairs on my arms started rising, forming a natural conduit that allowed the "juice" to travel toward my wrist. Mesmerized, I watched as blood began filling the vessels in my arms and hands. Finding no resting place, it ignited the nerve endings in my knuckles. Tingling spread through my fingertips.

Was it a primitive force? Perhaps. Primordial? Later, others would use all sorts of strange mutterings and excuses to explain this juice. Whatever you called it, it sizzled through my body and went straight to my head, intoxicating me, overwhelming me. It all seemed ludicrous. Mind over matter? Suddenly, it was there again. That single notion. One solitary idea. What if?

I was unable to squelch the idea, and my fingers began violently shaking. Frightened of being found out, I glanced furtively around, looking to see if anyone had noticed my unusual behavior. I was alone. Suddenly things reversed. The juice, as I now called it—it wasn't blood or emotion—began moving up my fingers, crawling over my wrist, and consuming my right arm. Simultaneously, my left arm began juicing, and I watched with a mixture of horror and excitement as it spread over my shoulders, paused slightly, then parted at my neck and spread. Racing uncontrollably, the juice poured into my chest, stomach, hair, legs, and feet. The sputtering flame was now gone—replaced by a fire that burned clean. The thought What if? had vanished. A single word throbbed in my brain; like a blossoming, white-hot pimple, it exploded on the mirror of my mind. *Murder.*

Upon reflection, I really don't know how I had gotten to that point. I didn't really care who I murdered or for what reason or provocation. Determination filled my heart— what little heart that still existed. The supernatural no longer permeated my life. Being angelic, I could not experience death—mankind's natural endpoint. That was beyond my abilities. Unnatural human actions were beyond the scope of my creation. I exceeded expectations.

I have been called many names since my first earthly manifestation. Reprobate. Demon. Tempter. Destroyer. Just to name a few. In the beginning, no one could fathom the meaning of such names. After what I did, I suppose it made sense — to them at least. But for me . . . I only saw pain. Does that surprise you? Elohim and Yeshua called it pride. I felt pain. Don't feel sympathy. I don't deserve it. I don't want it. My punishment was just and righteous. In fact, it was exactly what I wanted. Seriously, it put me right where I needed to be.

Having tasted the juice of bitterness, my body demanded more. My appetite grew by both measure and magnitude. The cup was blood. The bread was murder. I would eat and drink to the fullest.

I suppose you wish to know details? Fine. I will indulge you. I'm always willing to allow others to experience and admire my irrefutable intellect and dazzling superiority.

Some things stick to you, like a stain on your shirt. I'll never forget that burning, irresistible urge and the day I chose to act out my obsession.

It had been a warm spring day, and heaven was busy with activity. I too was scurrying across the rotunda, doing my daily duties. I had entered the council building and turned down a back hallway, where I saw a young angel, naively unaware of my grim determination, smile at me as he stepped to the side to let me pass. Faking a sincere smile, I moved past him, while the voice in my head screamed, *Now!* The juice pulsed through my veins. Now! This is it. Don't think. Let the juice flow.

With growing resolve, I pivoted, reversed course, and quietly approached him from behind. "Excuse me," I said, placing my hand on his shoulder. Startled, he turned toward me. I felt the bloodlust rise within me. Glancing around, I saw nobody. We were alone in the hall. Noting a small closet door directly behind him, I felt the juice rush once again over my entire body. I shuddered. What if?

"Can I ask you a question?" I stammered, hoping to lull him into lowering his defenses. Who wouldn't trust a stammering buffoon?

Disarmed, he smiled. "Sure!"

"Where can a guy get a clean trash bag?" Laughing slightly, I added, "Seems like a dude just can't catch a break."

Turning his head, he looked toward the closet. "Right here. Let me help you," he added.

"Would you? That's so awesome."

Grasping the handle, he turned the knob and opened the door to a broom closet loaded with supplies. He stepped in and began poking through items on the shelves. Moving silently, I pulled the door shut with my left hand while placing my right hand on his shoulder. Spinning him to face me, I reached out and grabbed his throat.

"What . . . " he gurgled as my grip tightened. My unexpected action, my unimaginable intention, left him helpless. What if? exploded into Do it! in my mind, and I felt my fingers dig deeper into the muscles of his neck in obedience. My thumbs found soft tissue, and I pressed harder and harder until I heard the crack of cartilage. Shocked by the sound, I hesitated. Instantly he fought to escape.

No. Now. Do it. What if?

Adrenaline surged through my body. The juice was flowing, and I was helpless to stop it. I didn't want to stop it. The hairs on my arm rose and twirled in the still air. Jolted back to reality, I heard the gurgle of air rasping over a broken larynx. Raising my gaze from his throat, I peered into the eyes of my victim. Once-vibrant brown eyes now looked like tiny dull voids as life drained from this nameless face. I waited patiently, and, as the last glimmer faded, I heard myself saying . . . "My name is Abaddon."

Some call me Satan, others Lucifer or the Prince of the Air. I was especially proud of what God's son, Yeshua, called me: Father of Murder. It was an accurate description. Cain, David, Saul, and countless millions would agree.

The present, after the Heavenly Council

Remembering that first time still thrilled me, but it was not enough just to remember. It certainly would not be the last time. Now Job, this new one, was on my mind and next on my list. I know what you're thinking; Elohim said no. But Job *will* fail and curse God. And when he does, the protection will be lifted, and in that precise moment, I will strike and crush the life from Job just as I did from that nameless face in the closet long ago. Just as I will do to anyone who professes to love God. Just as I did to his son, Yeshua.

Someday I hope my hands will find their way to a special place, a place where God himself is seated. Because, you see, that's what this is all about—the death of God and of everyone who claims allegiance to him. Stand in my way, and I will squeeze the life from your feeble body. Don't think I don't see you. I do. And when you least expect it, I'll be there. My name is Abaddon, and I am the father of murder.

IX

When tragedy strikes, we all have a choice to make;
we can choose to live in the shadows.
We can fling ourselves off the cliffs of death,
or we can humble ourselves
and call out to him—Elohim!

JOB
June 15, 11:45 p.m. • *Motel 6, Mission Valley, San Diego*

"Seriously?" A thick voice whispered into my ear, spraying drops of saliva. "You can't believe anyone cares about you or can help you."

My body bucked as I fought to tear myself away from this invasion of privacy. One hand gripped the back of my neck, while the other squeezed my head like a pair of pliers breaking a nut. Once again, I found myself staring into the face of Abaddon, this crazed maniacal devil. I'd thought I'd been hallucinating, just hearing voices. Just imagining that insane moment. Then I realized the voice whispering to me was real.

"You stupid, ridiculous, moronic crybaby. You do realize that I caused this suffering? I am the author of your pain." He paused to let the words sink in. "You cannot fight me and win. I will defeat you. And then . . . " A dramatic silence hung in the air. "I will kill you." The voice lingered over each of the last four words, dragging out each syllable like blood dripping slowly from the blade of a knife. "I . . . will . . . kill . . . you."

Only then did he release my neck, running his tongue hungrily over his dry lips. When he reached out his free hand, without thinking, I clasped hands with Murder. Grinning slightly, he flashed glaringly white teeth.

Yes, I am dead, I thought, but not dead as you imagine.

Shaking my head slightly, I tried to push away this strange mix of emotions. I wanted to pretend it didn't exist. The demons crawling through my nightmares. Slinking across my day, linking me with darkness. What did it all mean? Time froze as I stared at Abaddon. Was he reading my mind? Suddenly, I understood what he was doing. Maybe it doesn't make sense to you, but for me, it crystallized like boiling water flung into sub-zero temperatures. Without warning, the evil done by others can descend on us, bringing fear we cannot control. Silently, the ghouls pursue us in our sleep, leap out at us in the daylight, and seek to consume us in our darkness.

Rich or poor, simple or complex, inexplicably, we are connected by a thread that, paradoxically, makes us feel isolated. Its tendrils wrap tightly around our hearts and minds, while fear strangles the life out of the best of us. The worst of us. Every one of us.

• • •

JOB
June 16, 3:04 a.m. • Motel 6, Mission Valley, San Diego

Injuries and illness have plagued me all my life. I'm not injury prone, just injury riddled. Dog bite, snake bite, pneumonia, go-cart accident, multiple bike accidents, including riding into a parked car. Pain has haunted my physical body for decades. My first surgery was at age twelve. My fibula and tibia were shattered at age nineteen. Like mutton at the butcher's shop, my jaw was splintered into fragments following a basketball incident when I was 20. Blood poured like water within my thigh after my muscles were torn in a softball collision in my late twenties. Flash forward, and at age thirty, my appendix burst and was subsequently carved from my body. Most recently, they yanked my gall bladder through my belly button. But on this day, my skin felt as if it were on fire. Clawing like a cat trapped beneath a blanket, I ripped off my sheets and raced to the bathroom.

Splashing cold water over my burning face, I stared intently into the mirror and saw a weird reflection. Stunned by the view, I thrust my face even closer to the glass. My face and neck were splotched with bright reddish purple spots with angry white centers the size of nickels. Carefully, I pressed on a zitty-looking core on the side of my face. My finger felt heat emanating from the angry welt. Yelping, I yanked my hand away.

Dear God! What was this?

I pulled off my shirt and felt the fabric scrape blisters on my back. Dozens if not hundreds of angry red pustules covered my chest and back. Even without looking at my legs, I knew that I was completely covered in boils.

I've had zits in my day, but these were not ordinary pimples. I tried splashing cold, then hot water on them, but either way, it felt like acid rain, only making the pain burn even worse. The slightest touch turned the fiery circles into oozing volcanoes of pus.

I remember my doctor once saying that stress causes the body to do strange things. Our tongues thicken, our saliva dries, our nose plugs, our brain freezes, and our body begins to heat up. I was on fire, that much was true. Glancing into the water-splashed bathroom mirror, I decided I looked like a rotting carcass from a zombie show. "You can't make this up," I said out loud. "No way possible. I'm cursed."

Quickly, I retreated back under my sweat-soaked sheets. Lying quietly, I waited for the pain and panic spreading across my chest to subside. Anxious thoughts raced through my mind like scurrying rodents. Joy had called to tell me our older daughter was filing for divorce. My deepest fear for our family was becoming a reality. The cycle would continue. My wife's parents had divorced, my parents had filed after just four years of marriage, and while my wife and I had remained faithful, I was seriously worried about the toll the stress of these relentless attacks was taking on our marriage. And now my daughter—brokenness would once again mar our family legacy. I was having difficulty thinking rationally. This was my fault, Joy had told me. I was to blame. I never should have left my family to move out of state for business. If I had stayed, things would be different. I could have saved them. History teaches a subtle lesson: foolishness is the fate of those without faith.

I slipped from my bed to the cool tile floor. "God, save me!" The words escaped my lips unbidden. I lay there quietly, listening. But there was only silence.

Suddenly, without my even knowing how or exactly when it started, he was there.

"Job, why is your mind leaping from problem to problem?" The quiet voice made me feel instantly calmer in spite of the gentle chiding. "Your anxious thoughts snarl your mind into a tangle of frustration. Worrying is a choice that deprives you of the opportunity to live in the light and keeps you in a world of darkness. I long to touch you, but I will not violate your freedom to choose. I stand silently in the back of your mind, longing for you, waiting for you to call out to me. Remember, I am here."

My phone vibrated, and fear stabbed my heart. What was next? What else could possibly go wrong? How is it possible for something on silent to still be so noisy? Like a swarm of angry bees, the phone crept slowly across the end table, rattling as vibrating plastic and metal bumped along wood. It was a local number. I really didn't want to answer, but the preview screen grabbed my attention. Two words. Two simple but crazy, scary words: "Open me."

I did. As I pressed my thumb to the home button, I anxiously scanned the green box with the mysterious message. Holding my breath, I double tapped and read: "Do you like your new look? This is just the beginning. Next, I'm going to kill you."

The words scared the Beetlejuice out of me. I leaped to my feet, forgetting Elohim's words in an instant. Overcome with fear, I raced back to my old friend, worry. Finding no comfort, I paced the floor until it was time to go to the airport to fly home.

Where are you, Elohim?

X

True wisdom has perspective.
Those in Elohim's kingdom understand
that the purpose of life is not just
to be happy but to glorify him.

JOB
June 19, 8:53 p.m. • *Roadside Inn*

ALONE IN A CRAPPY HOTEL ROOM on the bad side of town, miles away from the what had been—until recently—my family's happy home, I took stock of my current state of affairs. My skin was covered with painful boils and oozing pus. My son was missing, and police still had no leads. My youngest children were sick with a mysterious illness. To make matters worse, my identity had been stolen, which had resulted in FBI agents raiding my family's home and confiscating our computers and cell phones. That was quite the story—with photos from the newspaper—for the family scrapbook! Through no fault of my own, all of my financial assets had been frozen. My hijacked Facebook and Twitter accounts besmirched my reputation with lies—steamy stories of alleged affairs and assorted sundries that had embarrassed my family and devastated my wife. And then there was the advice my wife had bitterly given me just before she left to stay with her mother: "Why don't you just curse God and die?" I couldn't blame Joy. I would have left me too. But I did blame her. It hurt so badly. Just when I needed her most. What happened to "for good and bad, richer or poorer, in sickness and in health"?

Now the house was gone too, and I had nothing left. Nothing but misery and self-recrimination. Glancing down, I was shocked to notice my broken, unkempt, dirty fingernails and my nasty, dry, cracking skin. Agitated, I drummed my fingers on the dark table upon which lay scattered what remained of an unsatisfying supper. Like a paste of dust and puke, my supper thickened in my mouth. Its repellent taste lingered on my tongue, and it smelled stale and bitter, giving me the impression of a mixture of sand and saliva.

Staring silently out the window at silhouettes of clouds moving across the pale-faced moon, I sensed I was staring into the face of God. I desperately wanted to be free, like those clouds drifting across the sky. I wanted it badly. Instead, I was gripped by this terrible new reality. I could feel my life slipping through my fingers, one piece at a time. There would be no salvation. Darkness was coming.

"When darkness deepens, where can one go to find strength?" I said aloud to no one. My breaking voice echoed the condition of my flesh.

There was no answer. I no longer heard Elohim. I was totally alone in the darkness. Wracked with pain, wallowing in self-pity, I wondered how to find meaning in things I could not understand. Why? I just wanted a simple answer to that question. I know the who. That's plain as day. But why? Tell me. That's all I ask.

Embracing my self-loathing and pity, I continued my mindless rambling. "I am not of this place, yet I walk its dusty gutters, hungering for a place to call home. And I have found no hope."

After a pause, I spoke again, hoping against hope that this time, my words would find a sympathetic ear and be answered. "Who can make sense of that which evades discernment?"

I laid my head down slowly, tears spilling from my eyes and splashing onto the table. After what seemed like hours, I stumbled to bed, praying for sleep—and escape.

A moment later—or was it forever—I woke to deep throbbing spasms of pain in my thighs. The sorry excuse for a bed I was sleeping on barely accommodated my six-foot frame, and my awkward positions had triggered muscle cramps. I held my breath and thrashed back and forth like an upside-down turtle as I kneaded my aching legs. A thought—it was an accusation, really—screamed in my brain: What next? My thoughts drifted as the pain finally subsided.

Slowly, I became aware of a light but steady tapping on my door—room 253 of this seedy motel—the only motel I could scrape together a few dollars to afford. Who the heck even knows I'm here? Instinctively, I reached for the miniature baseball bat standing beside my bed. It was my only weapon.

The insurance agent had called it "an insurance premium reduction." "If you buy this," he said, "I'll reduce the cost of your policy by 10 percent."

"What do you use it for?" I asked.

"To knock out a window if your house catches on fire. It's only $19.95."

Of all the stupid ploys . . . I had thought at the time.

"$19.95 for a mini-bat, and it doesn't even say "Louisville Slugger"? I had asked, working hard to keep my eyes from betraying my skepticism.

Joy had shot me a look warning me to behave and then mouthed, "We. Need. That."

Flash forward, and I was standing in my underwear ready to crack some skulls with my as-yet unused mini-bat. Weird, how we recall strange sequences in moments of panic. When Joy had left, I'd found the mini-bat standing in the corner where our bed used to be. She got the bed; I got the bat.

The tapping became heavy pounding, once again demanding my attention. Holding my bat like a Samurai sword, I swallowed hard and squeaked out, "Who is it?"

"It's me, Elliot."

"Elliot who?" I asked with suspicion.

"Elliot Haverstick." He paused, then continued. "How many Elliots do you even know? Seriously, you called me."

It was Elliot. Nobody could be that full of himself and full of manure at the same time. "It's a skill I have worked hard to perfect," he had often reminded me.

Smiling sheepishly, I popped the chain and slid the bat to the floor.

"Entré," I said, waving him across the threshold.

Elliot walked in, looked around the dingy room, and muttered, "You can't be serious, Jobski! This is a disaster."

I shrugged and, for the first time, he finally shifted his focus to me. "Glad you called! Surprised, but glad. What's up?" Shock was evident on his face as what he saw in my face started to register. "Dear God, what happened to you?"

"Oh, these little things?" I asked bitterly as I ran my hand lightly over my angry, burning chest. "They call them boils."

"Wow! I've never seen anything so hideous in my life."

"Thanks," I replied. Yet I couldn't help but agree. I shook my head slowly. "It's a mess, Elliot. The most insane, improbable story you'll ever hear."

"Well, first things first," he said, looking around. "I need a drink. And from the sounds of it, you'd better make it a double. Spill your guts, Jobi."

Elliot and I go way back. College, wedding parties, mayhem, stupidity, and lots of fun. Haver, as we dubbed him, was a true friend. But like most, we had drifted apart over the past few years—by mutual agreement. We still cared, but life had gotten in the way. Too much work for me, too much drinking for Elliot. Somewhere along the way, there had been a misstep, and our paths had diverged. Family, God, and work for me. Agnosticism, anger, and divorce for Elliot.

I studied him for a moment in silence, taking the measure of the man before me. "Can I trust you?" I asked. It completely broke conversational protocol, but time was short. Death was stalking me—perhaps even around the next corner. I didn't have time for trivial chitchat about sports or his personal exploits.

"Why wouldn't you?" Elliot asked, more curious than offended.

"Because . . . " I paused, as my eyes bored into Elliot, still sizing him up. "Everyone has betrayed me."

Cocking his head slightly, Elliot pushed his tongue to the side of his mouth and bit down on the inside of his lip. It was his trademark. I could see the wheels turning in his mind, one of the most brilliant I'd ever encountered. "How about this?" Nodding his head like a goofy bobblehead doll, he continued. "I'm a college professor. Right?"

He waited until I nodded, and then continued. "So, treat this like a debate. We each state our opinion. No advice, only rhetoric. Thus, we avoid any conflict of interest and minimize the potential for betrayal. Just pretend we're a couple of students arguing about life. The only thing at stake is our grade. What do you say?"

With a tired smile, I walked to the window and flung open the curtain. Moonlight spilled through the dirt-streaked glass into the darkened room. I motioned him to the chair by the window. "Make yourself comfortable, Sir Haver," I said. "This might . . . let me rephrase . . . this *will* . . . get ugly."

I stepped to the opposite wall, opened the fridge, pulled out a can of beer, popped the top, and handed it to Elliot. "I was ready for you." Reaching deeper, I grabbed a bottle of Diet Mountain Dew, twisted the cap, pulled a long draw, swallowed, plopped down in the faux leather chair that matched Elliot's, and began.

"There is only one story, and it's the story of darkness and light. The earth was empty. 'In the beginning, God created the heavens and the earth. And the earth was without form and void, and darkness covered the deep.'"

Sucking in a deep gulp of air, I continued. "Let me ask you a question, Elliot." My voice grew stronger as I laid out my thesis for Elliot. The question, while grammatically simple, carried implications of great consequence.

"Why did God—Elohim, as I call him—create darkness first?" Noting Elliot's puzzled expression, I elaborated. "Reflect for a moment. First, there was darkness. Then there was light. Strange." Elliot's expression changed to interest, and I continued. "Maybe, like me, you've never thought about it in those terms? First the dark, then the light. Quite the opposite to most rational human thought. Therefore, it stands to reason that darkness was around for an extended season, maybe longer than we care to imagine."

Glancing at my companion, I noticed a small grin playing at the corners of his mouth. Elliot was a drama king. He loved nuance . . . the roundabout, the cul-de-sac of shooting the breeze. Who was I kidding? I loved it too! Gathering my thoughts, I continued my presentation.

"From the darkness of my mother's womb, I came screaming into the world. Stark naked, my eyes open, I felt the kiss of life. Most are born devoid of hope. Others open their mouths and find riches in their first bite. Some might call me blessed. Me? I curse the day I was born. My worst fears have become reality. Drinking life's glorious splendor, I start to believe that this is life, in all its golden existence. Then reality strikes, and I realize it's all jabberwocky. How does this apply to you personally, my friend? Simple. Whether you believe it or not, you're not charmed every day of your life. Things will go badly, and when they do, you'd better be prepared for angst and pain. Alone, deep in the night, you'll strain for a hopeful sound. But it's like dropping a pebble of hope into a black hole; there is only silence."

Turning my gaze from the ceiling, I sought Elliot's eyes. "So, here is the satirical examination of my ill-suited logic. I believe this constitutes a more—shall we say—'realistic look at life.'" I made air quotes so that Elliot could better understand.

Elliot blinked and nodded slightly, signaling that he was following me. I continued, "Our outlook changes as we come to grips with why people experience evil in the course of life on earth."

Pausing for dramatic effect, I once again looked upward and said, "And thus my theory."

Rising from my chair, I curtsied like a ballerina and reached once again for the bottle of Diet Mountain Dew. Unscrewing the cap and placing my lips on the grooves, I guzzled. "Your turn," I said between slurps.

"You are so lame, dude," Elliot smirked. "Always with the Mountain Dew. Remember that time we walked to the top of the Golden Gate Bridge and you got to the top and pulled out a can of Mountain Dew and wanted a selfie?" Standing to his feet, Elliot rolled his back and stretched his hands to the ceiling. "Oh," he muttered, "it stinks to get old."

"Speak for yourself, you grizzled old mountain goat!" I quipped.

"Hush, you whippersnapper."

"Whippersnapper? What are you, eighty years old? I feel sorry for your students, having to endure your 1960s jargon."

"Fine." Elliot snapped, obviously stung. "Open your ears and hear the words of the great sage."

I nodded. "This should be good." Elliot was a good storyteller, but I couldn't give him the satisfaction of knowing I thought so.

He began, "Hearken back to a time not so long ago. To a night unlike any I'd ever experienced before. Deep, deep sleep had settled over me. Wracked with exhaustion, my mind cycled down level by level until only my eyes flickered under my twitching eyelids." Elliot quickly studied me to determine whether I'd picked up on his *Inception* movie reference. Satisfied that I had, he continued. "My skin cooled, but my pulse quickened as I breathed faster and faster. My body was asleep, but my subconscious opened like an oyster yielding its pearl. Suddenly, I was awake, lying face down. I felt the rough woven fabric of a couch that, somehow, I was sitting in. It took a second for my senses to catch up to my new reality. I saw nothing but darkness. Remaining silent, I carefully rolled onto my back. Then I heard it—a faint whooshing sound followed by several clicks. It sounded like clicks you'd make with your teeth and tongue. It seemed human, possibly supernatural, probably evil—all at the same time. Whatever it was, it was alive. Suddenly I not only heard but felt the whoosh. Air rushed across my face, the hair on my arms began to stand up, and a tingling sensation spread throughout my body. Instantly, I knew its origin. Death was surrounding me, as terror gripped me from head to foot. And then I heard an unknown voice speak: 'Do you believe, human? Do you believe that you are more perfect than your creator?'"

"Ha." I snorted. "This is movie-script stuff. What old Netflix show did you steal this from?"

"Shut your face, Job!" Elliot's dark green eyes locked with mine. He then said the words that made my stomach flatten and my tongue press against the roof of my mouth. "It was Abaddon."

Fear raced through my body. Exhaling loudly, I slumped backward in the chair.

"Oh," Elliot said matter-of-factly. "You know him too?"

I'd known fear. Or at least I thought I had. I'd been thrown into countless horrific situations as a CEO, husband, father, and son. They'd felt real. Perfectly real. But this *was* real, and beyond anything I'd ever experienced. My heart was thumping so hard that I wondered if I would drop dead of a heart attack. Things didn't look so bright. Was this the end?

"Let's get out of here," I said, suddenly feeling an irresistible urge to flee. "I don't think it's safe here."

"What do you mean?" Elliot asked.

"I told you, bro. People are after me. My life and anybody around me are in danger."

"Well, let's get outta here then. Besides," he paused for effect. "This room is a pit."

Glumly, I looked around and slowly nodded my agreement. "Yeah, it sucks."

"Where to, oh great leader?" Elliot twisted the door handle and opened the door just a crack. After cautiously glancing up and down the hallway, he carefully swung open the door.

"Uh . . ." I mumbled. "I'm broke. Seriously, I'm busted."

"No worries, brother, I can hook us up. I got a place in mind that's safe and has good food. You game?" I nodded my acquiescence.

Grabbing my bag, I stuffed my junk in it and quickly scanned the room one last time. I saw the bat. "Might need this!" I explained to Elliot.

"Ha! As if that could cold-cock a demon."

Funny, the tiny optimistic side of my brain was telling me that somehow, I just might get out of this alive after all. If only dreams could come true. The elevator dinged, and Elliot called out, "Let's go, Job." I swallowed hard, slammed the door shut, and raced down the hall.

"So where are we going?" I asked as we ran toward the elevator.

"Let's find Billy and Zeke," Elliot answered. "Reunite the old gang and see if they can make sense of this Mother Goose nursery rhyme of a story."

Great! I thought cynically. The old gang? Really? Still, I heard myself saying, "Great. I could use the help."

XI

Take heed of secret sins.
They will undo thee if loved and maintained:
one moth may spoil the garment;
one leak drown the ship; a penknife stab and
kill a man as well as a sword;
so one sin may damn the soul;
nay, there is more danger of a secret sin causing the
miscarrying of the soul than
open profaneness, because not so obvious
to the reproofs of the world;
therefore take heed that secret sinnings
eat not out good beginnings.

JEREMIAH BURROUGHS

JOB
June 19, 11:27 p.m. • *Lucky 13 Bar and Grill*

THERE'S A COMMON CATCHWORD: *It*. Businesses, nonprofits, even religions claim they have It. Some call it charisma. Many consider it personality.

Billy had It. Charm, gobs of personality, and plenty of charisma. My freshmen year, he had simply stuck his head in my college dorm room and said, "Hi, I'm Billy." Not many have the self-confidence to pop into a stranger's room and introduce themselves cold turkey. Far fewer have the nerve to face rejection at any level. Billy simply didn't care. Later, he would say, "I can't fix people's hang-ups, but I can brighten their day."

Sitting at a table in the Lucky 13 Bar and Grill, I wondered what had happened to that dreamy-eyed lad from college.

89

Staring at Billy across a stained, worn table covered with empty beer bottles, I now understood. Billy, as stained and worn as the table, looked weary and totally beaten down by life, as he seemed hellbent on drowning his misery with shots of Captain Morgan Spiced Rum.

It had begun one typical lazy fall Saturday when the love of his life, his wife of six years, had announced her love for another woman. Throw in the death of his mother by breast cancer, and two car wrecks that had brought lingering back and neck issues, and Billy had lost himself in a frenzy of drinking, parties, and soon-forgotten one-night stands.

Like good little soldiers, the rest of us plodded along, mindful of Billy's plight but either too scared to confront him about it or too frightened to admit our own vulnerability. Still, that night, seeing his face light up when he saw me and feeling how tightly he hugged me both alarmed me and, simultaneously, lifted my spirits. If anyone could understand my plight, it would be Billy, a fellow human beaten to a pulp—a whimpering man-child.

Aren't we all Billy? I thought as we sat down and ordered drinks. "Move me an inch closer to the cliff, and I'll fall off too," I murmured.

"What did you say?" Billy quizzed.

"Move over, big boy." I laughed. "Misery has company tonight."

"I can see that. What do you call those?" Billy grimaced, pointing at a seeping boil. "And is it contagious?"

"Has nobody ever seen a boil?" I laughed, wiping some pus with my index finger and threatening to smear it on Billy's sleeve.

After 40 minutes of catching up, Billy stood, placed his hands over his heart and said, "As the resident financial advisor and guarantor of all equations, I hereby announce that my quota of alcohol per my body mass has reached full capacity. I must recuse myself to yonder facility to relieve myself."

Stumbling slightly, Billy grabbed an empty chair for support.

"Elliot," I motioned, "go with him." "Yay, grand knight, your humble squire obeys your command."

"Shut up, you fool," Billy grumbled, "And help a tired old man to the potty."

I laughed quietly as the two of them left.

Man, this feels good, I thought. So good to be with friends. I could almost forget.

Moments later, Elliot, with Billy in tow, plopped down at the table again. "Just got a text," he said. "Zeke's walking in now!"

"Zeke?" I half shouted. "Good. We need a doctor. You two are a mess."

Everyone remembers the first verse of their favorite song. Like a bad karaoke night, we scream the first verse but make a mess of the second. Zeke was that forgotten stanza. You knew he was there, yet somehow, he blended into the background. A studious pre-med major, he had gone on to earn an MD and help save thousands of lives. The rest of us hoped only to save ourselves. He was a steady rock, a solid friend. Nobody was finer. While Billy, Elliot, and I all sang the same song, Zeke was always on a different verse.

Despite his money and respect, Zeke secretly battled a destructive addiction to pornography. When he'd been eight,

Zeke had stumbled onto his father's stash of girlie magazines hidden in the garage, and his mind had been forever altered. I was the only one in the group who knew. "Don't tell the others," Zeke had pleaded one night in his dorm room. Feeling vulnerable and convicted in a low moment, he'd openly confessed his "filthy habit."

From magazines to movies to the Internet, Zeke's addiction had progressed, raging hotter year after year. Listening and saying, "I'm sorry," had been my only response. What else does a twenty-year-old tell a confused peer?

Secretly, I'd been glad for the crack in Zeke's armor. Hiding my own insecurities seemed less difficult knowing that my friend was no saint. Don't get me wrong, I was concerned about him. Yet my support was no greater than that of a casual fan watching a ball game and screaming for someone to "catch the freaking ball!" Fast forwarding, porn had ruined his marriage. The secret was out; his wife had been devastated, and Zeke stumbled through life, for the first time uncertain of what was waiting around the next corner. I knew what lurked beyond that bend. Zeke was about to get introduced to Abaddon.

Still, just a couple of weeks ago, he'd begged me, "Don't tell the others, please!"

"Why?" I'd asked. "I don't get it. We all have our messes."

"Everyone but you, Job. You live a charmed life and, honestly, you never seem to make a mess of things. I don't know how you do it, but whatever you're drinking, I want it too."

"Zeke, my drink is Diet Mountain Dew. So grab a can, and let's be a mess together," I'd told him. How things had changed.

Turning away from the guys, I rolled my eyes and stuck my tongue out. If only friendship really mattered, I thought to myself. I would soon discover that all the kindnesses of friends mattered little when your own life was shattering in pieces. My eyes scanned around the table; Elliot, Billy, and Zeke, three people I'd known my entire life had a front row seat to the bloody mess I was making of my life.

XII

Elohim solemnly warns us there is no
middle, lukewarm, mamby pamby,
silly willy middle of the road. Live by faith,
not by sight. Totally in or totally out.

JOB
June 20, 3:36 a.m. • *Grand Hyatt Hotel*

IT WAS AMAZING how much ruckus four grown men could raise in a few hours. Zeke and Billy had long ago crashed in the penthouse suite graciously paid for by Elliot. Fitted with two personal hot tubs, multiple big-screen TVs, and the coup de grâce, the pool table of all tables, it was a setting for kings, not punks pretending to be royalty. With glazed eyes and foggy brains, we stared dully at images of yesterday's sports highlights. Elliot and I remained awake, if not fully alert. Neither of us spoke, which was fine with me. Drifting in and out of sleep, I knew I was ready to crash.

But then Elliot's slow, slurred words roused me from my stupor. "You know, Job. You're a pompous jackhole!"

"Shut up, Elliot," I slurred back, my tongue thick with exhaustion. "I don't want to hear your bull hockey! Just shut it."

Elliot was the most stubborn, mule-headed human I'd ever met. Ignoring my warning and acting like I didn't even exist, he continued his tirade.

"Why can't you just simply accept the fact you're a dirty rotten sinner like the rest of us and repent? You spent your whole life surrounded by yes people, and now I tell you the truth and you ignore me because I'm not perfect like you think you are. Let me add one more thing. If you sin, you get smashed. Believe me, I know! Firsthand knowledge of the truth from good ole Elliot."

His eyes flashed, and spit started collecting in the corners of his mouth. I averted my eyes, shook my head slowly, and let him continue on. There would be no stopping him anyway. Truthfully, I didn't give a toad's fart what Elliot said. My brain and body were mush from too much ice cream, greasy fries, and beef, and staring at three bloated pig men.

"Let me share what I've learned," Elliot droned on. "Think the bad dudes won't attack? Wrong. Darkness won't descend on your life? Again—wrong! Death isn't crouching at your door? Wrong. Wrong. Freakin' wrong!"

Turning, I looked at Elliot through narrowed eyes, not sure where he was going with this.

"It appears to me that we get what we deserve. The wicked may seem to go unpunished for a while, but eventually they receive their just desserts in life."

Now I was fuming, wide awake. And then he said it. The words that would forever alter our paths. Slicing through tendons, sinew, and muscle, plunging through bone, they broke me. "Job," Elliot said. "Face it. You are a failure."

I jumped to my feet, threw my head back, and screamed with such fury that light vanished and, temporarily, my sight.

"Wha . . . ?" Zeke's head suddenly appeared around the corner. "What the devil is all the noise?"

"Yeah," mumbled Billy, rubbing his crust-filled eyes. "Can you two stop being girlfriends for three seconds?"

"Let's play some pool," Zeke said, ambling over to the green velvet billiard table.

"Yeah," Billy said, following him. "I can't listen to this."

The stubborn anger refused to budge, eventually morphing into a dull ache of pain in my heart. Fumbling for words, I spoke, the words shaky from anger: "I didn't call together this little boy's trip. You guys did, so I don't care if you want to listen or not. It's my turn, and I've got something to say. Go ahead and play your game of eight-ball. Sit over there on your arse, Elliot, and drink your vodka. The rest of you, keep your yaps shut and your cauliflower ears open."

I knew it was a cheap shot, but I was ticked.

There was eerie silence, then a swift crack of pool balls and a squeaky fart from Elliot.

I shook my head, opened my mouth, and spilled my guts.

"Do you guys really believe that pouncing on me makes it safer for you? How many times have you walked into a bathroom and gagged on someone else's horrid stink only to later breathe in your own? The very thing you gripe and moan about ends up happening to you. Everyone is afraid of facing the truth, so we rip each other apart to escape the reality of our own pathetic lives."

My emotions slowly calmed, and I silenced my tongue. Seizing the moment, Billy leaned on his pool stick and took his turn.

"So what you're saying, Job, is that if I get mad enough, cry enough, or gripe enough, I can alter the reality of my world? I'm curious as to why you think getting angry or whining will change anything. I mean, stop and think. Evil befalls you and your family. Everything you know, everything you hold precious—'my precious,'" Billy croaked, attempting a weak imitation of Gollum from *Lord of the Rings*, "vanishes!" A small grin played across his lips. "And you whine just like the rest of us."

Elliot snorted in laughter. Glaring, I silenced him with my wrath-filled eyes. Gulping, he looked away. Billy continued in his ignorance. Good ole Billy, so puffed with pride. A man I both loved and loathed.

"Stop and think about it, bro," Billy said. "It all happened for a reason. I hate to say it."

"But you will," I retorted hotly.

"Yes, I will. As much as it pains me to say it."

"Come on Billy," I prodded him. "Tell me why. Give me one of your great Billy pearls. You know so much. Why did all of this happen to me? Why?"

"Yeah." Elliot quipped. "Tell us, you *hombre más fuerte*, you intellectual giant."

Knocked off course slightly by the stinging venom, Billy paused and then quietly offered, "Maybe this happened because you refuse to admit your secret sin. Or sins? Maybe, just maybe, Elohim wants you to repent."

Have you ever been so mad at something someone said to you that your brain just snaps shut? No snappy retort, no stinging sarcasm, no biting reply springs from your lips. You choke under the pile of dung dropped on top of your head.

I saw flickering black shadows as I pressed my hands over my tightly closed eyes, hiding my face. Fighting emotion, I considered my next course of action. Should I swallow hard and refuse to justify myself to them? Or should I rise with the fury of a tiger and plunge a knife into the eye of every one of these weasels who call themselves my friends?

Sighing deeply, I stepped to the side of the room; there simply was no excuse for this hurtful, hypocritical, childish behavior. Yet I reached for a cue stick leaning against the wall, knowing I was going to do something unforgettable I'd soon regret. Squeezing the stick in my sweaty palms, I whacked it on the edge of the pool table, snapping it like a toothpick between my fingers. Shards of wood splintered and flew into the ceiling and the green velvet of the Brunswick table. What I didn't anticipate was the stick shearing in half, sending splinters into the bottom of my hand.

Zeke gasped; Billy cursed. Elliot, smooth as a morning shave, calmly snatched a dish towel off the counter and, without saying a word, tied up my hand. Trembling, I glanced at it. I was shaking from shock. Blood was running into my upturned palm and dripping casually onto the wood floor. The shattered stick rocked gently on the floor as I panted quietly, wheezing in shallow breaths through my suddenly dry throat.

"Maybe we need to take a break?" Elliot said, continuing to wrap my hand.

"No way!" I screamed, launching the wild spittle of a madman into Elliot's startled face. Zeke and Billy tried to avoid my wrath and my notice, slinking to the nearby couch for refuge.

"You invited me to this masquerade ball, and I have yet to remove my mask and reveal my true identity," I said fiercely. "I'm cutting my own tongue off, so don't let this sacrifice be in vain."

Backing up slowly, Elliot eyed the broken stick, clearly wondering whether I might continue my violent rampage. Maybe he should have been afraid, but instead of lunging toward him, I backed up and leaned against the wall.

I looked around the room, making eye contact with each of them. "I think we have forgotten Elohim's grace," I said softly, and I could see the three of them relax slightly. "Good thing I'm not Elohim," I continued, growing louder, "or I would command the earth to open and swallow the whole lot of you." They tensed again, and I grew even louder. "Good thing, because I would just love to order a batch of poisonous snakes to slither across the floor and bite the crap out of every one of you."

Putting my head down, I noticed the dish towel turning red with my fresh blood. I laughed, throwing my head back, as the oddest thought crossed my mind. Not caring if they thought I was crazy, I spoke the words out loud: "Tell yourself, Duckie, you're really quite lucky." Relishing their confused discomfort, I added the attribution: "Dr. Seuss."

Sighing deeply, I struggled to express my next thoughts. "Sometimes, boys, you never find out what Elohim is doing. That's part of the package, whether you like it or not. Sometimes you get lucky and get to open the shiny box. Other times, all you can do is shake it and dream of the prize." Aware of the blood pooling in my hand, I suddenly felt light-headed and desperately wanted to find a bathroom. Without uttering another word, I walked to the bathroom, my bloody hand dripping all over the floor.

XIII

*Scream, kick and throw a hissy fit, but in the end,
you will either beg for the gun in your mouth
or beg Elohim for mercy and hope.*

JOB
June 20, 4:03 p.m. • *Denny's*

COCKING MY HEAD SLIGHTLY, I stared awkwardly at a bleached splotch of paint three feet above everyone's heads in the back corner of the neighborhood Denny's. It's amazing what a good night's sleep, seven stitches, and a late afternoon breakfast can do for the mind and body. Leaning back in my chair, I rocked on two legs, tempting fate—and a concussion. I rolled my head, trying to relax my aching neck muscles; feeling little comfort, I sucked in a quick breath of air and tried to rouse the attention of my dejected friends. "Let me tell you a story."

"Go for it, Job," said Elliot. "I'm listening." Seeing no defensive postures, I began.

"The air is still. No movement awakens my senses. Yet every nerve is sensitized. I sit alone. My meager shadow is my only friend. The heat is stifling. Thick dust floats in the air. My eyes dart furtively across the rolling valley of trees and rocks. Opening my mouth, I extend my swollen tongue, searching for sensation. Although I can't feel, smell, or see him, I know he's there, ready for the kill shot. My adversary lies hidden beneath the mossy underbelly of a distant hill, watching, waiting. Caught in the sniper's crosshairs, I imagine him locked on my forehead. Breathing silently, I hear the faint click, click, click of the trigger and the soft thump of the bullets traveling through the barrel. A bullet named Job blazes a path toward my head. Sensing the end, I close my eyes. No longer watching. Just waiting. Waiting in silence for the bitter end. The bullet pierces my skull, and all sound and motion is immediately extinguished. A light shimmers. I see a throne. Elohim stretches out his hand. Fade to black."

I let them think about that for a moment before continuing. "I know we visited this last night," I said, "but sometimes—like cold hash browns for breakfast—it's all we've got on the table. Sitting on the pot this morning, I concluded that I've actually done nothing to deserve this ridiculous treatment. Whether you believe it or not, I've lived a pretty sinless life."

I stood slowly and began pacing the room like a wolf prowling for prey. Avoiding eye contact, I began my attack. "So, Billy, how much money do you have in that offshore account?"

"What the . . ."

"Oh yeah, we know. All of us know. Just in case . . . what? Your marriage goes south? Or one of your business deals turns a little sketchy?"

"Elliott . . . " Once again, I paused dramatically. "Let's see. Hard to believe you once did Bible Quiz, Fine Arts, and Youth Camp all in one year. Mister I'm on fire for God. Gonna be a world changer. Just look at you now. Mister agnostic. Mister skeptical of everything religious, never finishing anything and always disgusted with everyone."

Picking up speed, I began circling the room faster and faster, the anger and pain spilling on each of my "friends." Faster—as if I could escape their pain. Faster—as if I could escape my own.

"And last but not least, Zeke. What to do with that secret porn addiction? Hard to balance a life of church involvement with spending time looking at Internet porn, isn't it? Yeah. I would have to say, relatively speaking, I'm doing pretty good."

Rounding the circle one last time, I realized how quiet it had become in the room. Screw it. I had come this far. Might as well go for the jugular. Finish this puppy off. Heading for the exit, I stopped and looked at them. My so-called friends. I heard small sniffles from behind Zeke's hands, which covered his face. Billy stared at me defiantly; I arrogantly smiled right back and glanced at Elliot, who stared at the ceiling as if willing it to fall and bury him alive. Or so I thought. What did I know, anyway? This had been a colossal waste of time and energy.

"I'm taking a break," I told them, turning to leave. I'm going to get some fresh air and a cold Diet Mountain Dew.

Don't join me. Oh, and one final thing before I go." I dropped my gaze to the brownish gray, weirdly patterned carpet and proceeded earnestly: "Even after all of us have turned to dust, I'm still going to trust Elohim. He will stand upon this earth and rule in power. After my skin has rotted from my bones, even as a skeleton, I will look upon him. Me. Yes, me. I can't speak for you. But I hope you too want to behold him in all his glory. I really do." Pausing not for effect but from deep emotion, I added, "I want nothing in return. Just his presence and grace."

With that, I turned the doorknob, slipped from the back room full of stunned faces into the quiet restaurant, and headed for the street.

Walking, unaware of my surroundings, I felt my adrenaline begin to ebb and fear of the unknown taking its place. Shuffling my feet along the sidewalk, I reminded myself of a zombie lurching across the pavement.

My fascination with *The Walking Dead* was legendary. I didn't talk incessantly, dress up, or watch *Talking Dead* like the crazies. Nonetheless, those who knew me saw the obsession. Occasionally, I pondered what it would be like to be physically alive but mentally dead. My favorite video clip was one of a lone man in a tattered black suit stumbling through a scorched yellow field of withered grass and broken stalks of grain. Oblivious to the cars racing down the ribbon of road, he lurches slowly, arms flailing, coat flapping, and head flopping.

I had always imagined myself driving down the road of life in complete control of my own future and faculties. Not once had I seen myself as the man in the field, yet here I was, stumbling, bumbling, crumbling through an endless field of loneliness and pain.

Everyone was dead wrong. Every argument ever uttered, each written or verbal description lent credence to the complexity of walking but actually being dead.

Now I understood. Touched by pain, addled by misery, my body was moving, but I was dead inside.

XIV

If you know the enemy and know yourself,
your victory will not stand in doubt;
if you know Heaven and know Earth,
you may make your victory complete.

SUN TZU, THE ART OF WAR

JOB
June 21, 10:22 p.m. · *Christian Life Center parking lot*

THE ONLY THING between me and a cold park bench was a tank of gas and my rental car. I sat alone in a darkened parking lot, praying for hope, searching for peace, begging for mercy.

Laying my head back, I groped for the power seat button and released it. I reclined deeper and deeper into the crackling leather; lower and lower into the abyss of fear and hopelessness. Despair swallowed me like a pool of oily black tar. In spite of the drama playing out inside my car, all seemed normal from outside. No one would have looked twice at a random car parked in a deserted church parking lot. Outside the church where I'd once stood with hundreds, clapped my hands, raised my arms, whispered prayers, and worshiped Elohim.

Tonight, I sat silent, desperate, and supremely alone. I could feel it coming; I was on the edge of a severe anxiety attack. I'd had plenty of them the past few months, and I was intimately familiar with what they looked and felt like. Reclined in my seat, I thought back to my first experience of losing control and slipping into uncontrollable anxiety.

My oldest daughter is divorcing, and I'm concerned that my two precious grandchildren will be as vulnerable as lambs surrounded by ravenous wolves bent on ripping their flesh to shreds. I feel like a puny, helpless bystander. My wife and I have tried throwing money at the situation. We've cried; we've consoled; we've screamed; we've ranted; we've raved. Nothing save Elohim's intervention is going to fix this problem. Save the world? Didn't matter when I can't even save my family.

Mix in a heavy burden at work, plenty of bills, ridiculous weather—I'm feeling overwhelmed by the torrential rain of a hurricane of affliction. And then it happened—the nail in my coffin, the belt across my back, the boot up my butt, the straw that broke the camel's back. What was this decisive blow that finally pushed me over the edge? Misty—my faithful, sweet little dog who'd loved me for eleven years—died. Don't judge me. Until you've lost a pet you've loved for more than a decade as you've teetered on the brink, don't judge.

Thinking about it now, relaxed in this cold black leather car seat, I can understand that it hadn't really been the death of my dog that plunged me to the depths of despair, although she had been a comfort through some of the darkest days of my life. Misty's death was merely the ah-ha moment— the grim reality that my capacity to juggle sorrows had been exceeded. I had reached my limit . . . overdrawn my account . . . my reserve tank had run dry.

Suddenly, without warning, I was plunging off the bridge of my life, hurtling through space into a deep, dark lake of fear and uncertainty. Psychologists say that anxiety can manifest differently for each individual. A feeling of impending doom can be accompanied by trembling, sweating, a pounding heart, and other physical symptoms. My anxiety begins with my skin tightening, causing increased blood flow, which produces flashes or throbs of pain in my head, arms, legs, and chest.

Black spots obstructed my vision, but most troubling were the overwhelming and frightening disorienting thoughts of doing serious harm to myself. My life was imploding. Irrational thoughts—dreams of horrible, strange, and diabolical things I was convinced were going to happen to me, my family, and my friends—haunted me. Suicide not only began to seem like an option; terrifyingly, it was starting to seem like the only option. What if I took one last drive on the highway—felt the wind on my face and saw the familiar places one last time—and suddenly steered my car headlong into an oncoming giant truck, I wondered. If I hurled myself off this cliff, would I fly?

My anxiety leads to—and is worsened by—sleep deprivation. No matter how hard I try, I just can't shut down my brain and silence the endless, noisy stream of daily data. I would have doubted that I was sleeping at all, but the frequent nightmares that woke me up sweating or screaming belied that. Either way—sleepless nights or night terrors—I was a mess.

My eyes are closed, but I am wide awake. Shifting black shadows float across the darkness under my eyelids. The breath escaping my mouth sounds ragged.

An itch, a warm creeping rash spreads like a drink spilled on a table. Running toward the edges, it splits into two streams. The first streaks down both sides of my back, reaches my butt, and continues toward my toes. The second runs around my hips, zips up my spine, circles my neck, and climbs to the tip of my auburn hair. Feeling like a piece of raw meat stewing in a Crockpot, I fight to cool the heat, the itch. Rising in frustration, I bolt from my bed and race to the shower. Stripping off my cotton T-shirt and soaked underwear, I step into the coldest water my skin can stand. Shivering like a wet puppy caught in a downpour, I pound my fists on the shower wall to release my anxiety.

Turning off the water, I reach for a towel, dry myself off, fumble for clean clothes, and flop down on top of sheets still damp with sweat. Inhaling deeply, I force the air back out through a small gap in my taut lips. Rolling to my side, I punch my pillows and beg Elohim for sleep. "Please, just a few hours!" A dry cough slips from my mouth, and I reach for my bottled water; taking a tiny sip, I glance at my alarm clock—1:14 a.m.

I learned to play head games, distracting my mind, luring my body to sleep. That first time, I imagined myself staring at an elevator. The charcoal-colored door dinged as it opened. Stepping inside, I pressed my back against the cold handicap bar and lay my head against the woodgrain paneling lining the upper half of the carriage. The lights were dim, not harsh like an ordinary elevator. Smiling slightly, I relished the darkness as the faint whir of wheels and pulleys signaled my slow descent. In time, order was restored, and a deep euphoria spread through my mind. All that mattered was sleep.

Faster than a crack of lighting in a storm, the elevator leaped upward, surging with a blur of speed, seeking a new destination. My head banged against the panel, and I felt the metal bar smash into my lower back. Helpless to stop the rise, I braced for impact as the elevator exploded into space. Then I awoke, bitterly disappointed that I was still conscious. Rolling over, my eyes found the alarm clock; 1:22 a.m. Moaning in frustration, I figured the math; the realization that I'd been asleep for eight whole minutes felt like a slap across the face. Disoriented, yet lucid, lying in utter darkness, supremely alone, I felt the itch spreading across my body once more.

I blinked my eyes, and my pupils slowly adjusted to the darkness around me in my present reality. So much had changed since that first anxiety attack but, really, nothing had. Sitting in my car alone in the church parking lot, I recognized that familiar itch rising with my panic. I suddenly realized I was freezing cold. I fumbled for a blanket lying in the passenger's seat and tucked it tightly around my shivering body, pulling it up to my glassy, sleep-deprived eyes. Peering into the darkness, I heard the howl of the wind whipping through space. The sound did nothing to soothe the fire in my back. Maybe my wife had been right; maybe I should just curse Elohim and die. I would not be missed or mourned—just forgotten in the silence.

Yell a loud no to the Devil and watch him scamper.
Say a quiet yes to God and he'll be there in no time.

JAMES 4:7 MSG

ABADDON
June 22 • Location unknown

ABADDON SWORE SOFTLY. Before him lay the evidence of a night gone bad. Extremely bad. The stench of vomit and reefer permeated the atmosphere. Abaddon paced the room, his feet dragging across the worn carpet, emitting small balls of fuzz that floated aimlessly across the floor. His hands fluttered, his body twitched, his mind raced.

"How do I kill this Job?" he muttered. "Think! There must be a way."

Stopping dead in his tracks, he whispered, "Fear. Of course. Unadulterated, spine-tingling, wet-your-pants fear."

• • •

JOB
June 22 • Location unknown

Job sat in a shabby room of a seedy hotel on a street of bail
bond dealers, cheap nightclubs, and sour-smelling food
shops. A rickety chair uncomfortably held his exhausted
body. He stared at a collection of pizza boxes, crumpled cans,
and scattered candy wrappers that littered the place.

A trickle of musty lukewarm air blew weakly from a noisy
window unit. The bed was ancient, the sink and tub rust-
stained, the carpet frayed and worn. Clamping his hands to
the side of his face, Job absentmindedly rubbed his throbbing temples.

"How do I get rid of this Abaddon?" he muttered. "Think,
man, there must be an answer!"

Job rose quickly, the chair groaning under the release of
pressure. "Fear of God," he whispered, "Holy of holies. Lip-
burning, fire-in-your-belly fear of God!" What if Abaddon
believed Elohim would actually condemn him to hell?
Does Abaddon even fear God? Was this a hopeless exercise,
designed only to hasten my death?

The vibrating phone buzzed faintly in Job's pocket. He
pulled it out and read "Unknown." This development was
like sweet honey to a ravenous bear. Job touched "Accept"
and quietly said, "Hello."

"Job. It's me. You didn't really think I'd forgotten about
you, did you?"

Job's eyes froze, his blood cooled, and his heart skipped a beat.

"Run, Job," Abaddon taunted. "It's more fun when the prey turns chicken."

In spite of the provocation, Job kept silent.

"What?" Abaddon pressed him. "Nothing to say? It doesn't matter. I'm going to kill you anyway."

Courage rose from somewhere deep within Job, and he fired back, "Elohim won't let you."

"Actually . . . " Abaddon said slowly, carefully enunciating each word. "He said I can't kill you *now*. But how long is now? Let's play a little game." Now Abaddon sounded downright gleeful. "It's called Threat or Die."

Silence hung in the air as Job felt his courage fade.

"Oh, so sad, little Job. The cat has your tongue," Abaddon mocked. "Never mind. I'll go first. Threat or Die. Do you choose death or the threat of losing your family?" He paused and let Job consider the awful choice. "I'll see you tonight."

The phone went dead.

XVI

*Misery loves company,
but company does not reciprocate.*

ADDISON MIZNER

JOB
June 22

PACING THE DARKENED HOTEL ROOM like a tiger caged behind steel bars, I looked for ways to redeem the time. Bored out of my skull with *King of Queens* reruns, Angry Birds, and stale books, I'd taken to recording my thoughts — for the kids, my wife, maybe my friends? No one would probably ever listen to the mutterings of a self-professed Mad Hatter, but like an addicted sugar junkie, I indulged once more. Hitting the record button, I launched into the next download of my self-titled podcast, "The Dark/Light Chronicles." Slipping into my radio voice, I began.

No matter how you slice it, waking from a bad dream is one of the most frightening moments for the human mind and body. Scientists have attempted to explain the process. Psychologists

129

have studied it thoroughly, from the moment panic begins spreading through the limbs until it finally leaves the brain. It's a moment of complete incoherence sandwiched between questions like, Am I dead or alive? Was it real or fantasy? A memory? Or snapshot of the future? A nonsensical random twist or a flare of truth?

Each night, my mind paints using the same color wheel. Bolting straight up from the bed as if a leg cramp were seizing my muscles, wide awake, I clench my teeth and moan in fear. Rocking slowly forward and back like a madman writhing in a corner, I wait for the panic to subside and normalcy to return. After a few minutes, I pad to the bathroom, relieve myself, and return to my empty, cold bed.

I know it was for the best. That's what I told my wife. We pretended by saying, "It's not safe. I can't risk you and the kids getting hurt," and, pausing, I looked away and thought, Or killed. But the truth stood dark and silent, like the Ghost of Christmas Future. We both knew what was really happening. Life was jacked up. I was a disaster, and she didn't want a piece of my mess. So she left. How I missed seeing her brownish-blonde hair flowing over the tightly wrapped sheets that revealed her beautiful body, tightly cocooning her soul and mind in things more pleasant than I could offer her at the moment. Wrapped in slumber, her soft breathing would lure me back to sleep. But not tonight. I was alone.

Exhausted, I flicked off the record button, punched the bedstand light to bring darkness, sighed, and laid my throbbing head on a sour-smelling, lumpy pillow. This was no Grand Hyatt.

Life whirled busily just outside my four walls, but in my forgotten prison, it slowed to a barely discernible pulse. Never beginning, only ending, it replayed its sad refrain.

Softly at first, then louder, growing in intensity, never missing a beat. Never skipping a syllable, it faded like a last refrain echoing in an empty room. Listening quietly, I relaxed, and sleep returns to my tortured body.

I awakened to hands around my throat. Not just my throat but my arms and legs. Trussed like a pig for market, I was in a human straitjacket. A sweaty palm was clamped over my lips. I was unable to speak. Fighting was not an option. Slowly, I allowed my eyelids to flutter open, but all I saw were shadows and faint figures. Stale onions and cigarette breath tainted the air. I felt the urge to vomit but bit back the rising bile.

The faint glow of my bedside light cast shadows that flitted across the walls and ceiling. I understood. The room was filled with assailants. The realization sparked rising panic. Struggling to breathe, I coughed, simultaneously thrust my body upward in an attempt to free myself. Bony fingers deepened their probing, pressing harder, separating my muscles, tearing at my bones. Nerve-jangling pain ripped through my exhausted frame.

"Relax, Job, and this won't get any uglier."

Instant recognition flashed in my mind. I knew the voice. I had seen the face. The same face grinning at me in the coffee shop when this all started. The same face leering from the gray SUV chasing me. The same smug, arrogant jerk who strolled into the heavenly council with Elohim and laughed at his angels. Abaddon had returned, and there were no pretenses. There was no escape.

Suddenly, I questioned whether any of it had been real. It felt real, but how could any of this possibly be? Was it all just a dream? The fingers crushing my larynx loosened slightly, which allowed garbled words to escape my mouth. "Am I dreaming?"

"Depends on your definition of dreaming," the voice responded. "If you're talking a sunny daydream—strolling through the park with your lovely bride on your arm—" he paused dramatically, "then no. But if you're thinking, This is my worst nightmare come to life, like Freddy Krueger with death in his hands—then yes."

I felt the rush of his breath flowing into my mouth. Sickened, I tried to turn my head, but powerful hands once again crushed my neck muscles. Pressed beyond my ability to resist, I was forced eye to eye with my sadistic tormentor. Our lips touched; icy-cold breath poured into my mouth and escaped through my nostrils.

"Yes indeed," he practically spit. "Now that's a dream worth remembering."

Fear settled into the deep places of my mind. Finding no solace, it settled in my bones. Although I fought, I could not win. So I succumbed, and like a frightened child under the blankets, I involuntarily squawked like a plucked chicken.

"Poor puny Job." He jeered. "All alone and forgotten. Are you afraid of the big, bad wolf, Job?"

Lying still, I allowed his words to rush over me like storm water racing to the drain. "Do you feel it? The greasy, slimy tendrils of fear advancing through your veins?"

Don't weep or beg, I told myself, fighting emotion. Don't weep or beg. Even though I feared for my life, I could not—I would not—give him the satisfaction. But no words registered. I was powerless to utter a single, solitary word of defiance or capitulation.

My will to survive was ebbing. If this was the end, I was ready. Life is the only thing I had left to give. Everything else had been taken from me, so why fight?

"Get him up," the voice suddenly said to someone other than me. "It's time to go." Rough hands wrestled me to a standing position. Jerking my head back, I gazed again into those deep pools of blackness. I was face to face with Abaddon himself. He smiled and said, "I don't succumb to fear; I create fear."

In that exact moment, all systems burst to life. I don't know if it was his words, his arrogance, or his weirdly offensive breath, but suddenly, a blazing fire burst within my soul and ignited my spirit. Mustering my last ounce of energy, grunting in pain, I defiantly announced what was growing stronger in my heart "Though he slay me, I will not lose hope in him."

The only response was a sound—I heard it before I felt it—a faint whooshing, like a bat flying through air. Stars exploded before my eyes, but I felt no pain, no fear. Consciousness receded. Darkness was my new friend.

Silhouettes danced across the ceiling. My crust-matted eyelids flickered once, then twice. A dank, musty odor lingered in my nostrils. Raspy gurgles escaped my burning throat. Struggling to breathe, I coughed, and my depleted body demanded water. My mind screamed for answers. Where was I? Was my family safe? What did Abaddon want from me?

· · ·

JOB
The next morning

I had never before seen a therapist, but when you think you're going insane, you consider things you once found inconceivable. My latest obsession was dreams. More specifically, as described by my therapist, a multilayer sequence dream. The explanation goes something like this. You dream the same dream once or twice a week, and each time, you move the story along. Sequence by sequence. Layer by layer. Inch by inch. It never really ends, because your mind or subconscious doesn't know how to end the dream. It doesn't make sense. Like, you are back in high school and. . . . Only you graduated high school thirty years ago. Or you fight with your spouse, but you aren't married. In other words, the dream doesn't comply with your present reality. You will never understand or finish the dream.

Multilayer sequence dreams. Call it what you want. You can giggle behind my back. But truthfully? I don't care. All I know is, every time I crawl into bed, my thoughts quicken. My pulse races. I close my eyes, and I can feel the panic exploding like acetylene gas. It obstructs my vision and deepens my fear. I'm scared. Scared to open my eyes and see his face. To see those eyes. Those dark orbs of raw hatred glaring at me.

Darkness has a face. Terror has a smile. Fear has a name: Abaddon.

XVII

The question is not why.
The answer is simply YES!

JOB
June 24, noon • *Grand Hyatt*

BUBBLING WATER CASCADED from a nearby fountain, splashing my bare legs. A palm-frond roof nearby the cabana at the Grand Hyatt fluttered in the warm breeze. After our small group's disastrous encounter four days ago, I'd simply vanished. But Zeke was persistent, and I was a glutton for punishment, so I had agreed to another intervention. However, my good humor for these "Save Poor Job" charades was ebbing fast.

They were all there—Zeke, Elliot, Billy—along with a new kid, Eli. I'd met Eli, a protégé of Zeke's, a few times before. It seemed that Zeke had called in "fresh meat" for his "fish fry." But the purpose of Eli's being here didn't matter to me; he was just another tormentor with a vain smile and empty words.

"Where's the waiter?" Billy complained. "I'm thirsty." A handful of crumbs were scattered across the woven bamboo table.

"I hate these tables," I said. "They cut up your arms if you lean on them."

Looking like scared birds hoping to avoid the notice of a nearby serpent, my companions remained quiet.

Once again, Zeke was paying for this four-star spread. Paying made him feel special, even if it cost him a small fortune.

"Seriously, where's the waiter?" Billy whined. "I want steak and lobster."

Wasting no time, Zeke leaned back, smiled somewhat unconvincingly, and said, "Thanks for coming, everyone. I know you're busy, but this is important."

"Busy! Scratching our butts and sending emails? What a joke," I grunted.

"I've been giving this some thought," Zeke continued. "I believe history clearly proves that evil people and wrongdoers come to a swift, sudden, and well-deserved end."

Knowing instinctively that Zeke had simultaneously judged me and justified himself based solely on our current circumstances, I barely managed to restrain a flash of fierce anger. "What a load, Zeke!" My voice exploded across the pool plaza. "Common sense tells us that punishment is not meted out to the wicked nearly as often as you would like to believe. In fact, most of the time, wicked people never get caught." I paused and let that sink in. I stared Zeke in the eye until he looked away, uncomfortably. "None of you can show me how I've sinned," I continued. "And yet my life is a shambles. So, am I wicked or just a hidden sinner?"

"What's your point, Job?" Zeke snapped.

Pausing, I looked around at each of them while taking deep, measured breaths. It seemed clear that they believed their cause was just and they were doing me a favor by convincing me of my own sin. "Simple," I finally responded. "If even one godless, sin-riddled heathen prospers in this life, then your whole argument folds like a house of cards.

"Answer me this," I continued. "Why do the wicked prosper, grow old, and gain power while God-fearing, decent, humble, and innocent people are cut down in their prime?

"I'll tell you why. On this earth, evil wins. And his name is Abaddon."

With reckless abandon, I knew I was flirting with blasphemy, secretly ready to blame God for the world's brokenness. Eager to cast my stones of judgment, I momentarily studied the faces of my so-called friends. Did my angry, satirical tone of voice reveal the betrayal I was feeling within?

But at that moment of extreme exposure, I stepped back from the cliff of despair, the chasm of pain, and begged for mercy. "Elohim!" I cried out loud, sobbing. "Please help me!"

Then I felt it. It started as a faint whisper, but soon a stronger breeze of growing power spread over me. My mind grew calm. Opening my tightly closed eyes, I saw him, yes *him*, sitting in the empty, rose-colored lounge chair beside me. The plaza was empty. Everyone had vanished. Now it was to be man vs. God.

I slipped from my chair and dropped to my knees. "Elohim, I have failed you," I confessed, head bowed, voice quavering. Desperate, I pressed on. "My world is in ruins. I have lost my way. Fear has consumed my joy. Anxiety is my constant companion. I would understand if you chose to take my life. I deserve to die." Gathering every ounce of remaining courage and resolve, I steeled myself to utter what I supposed would be my last words: "No matter what, Elohim, I believe in you."

Suddenly, I was back in the plaza, and everyone else was there. What happened next still astonishes me to this day. Crazy storms are normal in the Midwest. Growing up on a farm, I saw tornadoes shoot out of thin air and rain sheeting so hard it turned sideways. But when Elohim shows up in California, he shows up big. Huge. Crazy. Scary big. One minute a gentle breeze was bumping the cabanas, then without warning, golf-ball-sized hail was being hurled from the sky. No lightning, no thunder, but raindrops the size of quarters descended from clear blue skies. Wind exploded, swirling the hail in spirals like cyclones. Buffeted by water, hail, and wind, the pool transformed into a turbulent, roiling pot. Geysers of water shot upward like water tornados, sending tables, chairs, and umbrellas flying across the pool plaza.

Sixty seconds might not sound like a long time, but in the midst of such chaos, it seemed like forever. My boxing coach had always screamed at me, "You can do anything for sixty seconds." Wrong. But by the grace of God, no human could survive a God-created cataclysmic event like we experienced for even thirty seconds. Sixty seconds—of hail ricocheting like shotgun blasts off glass tables and chairs, winds so strong they suck the air out of your lungs, and rain so hard it bruises the skin on impact—is an eternity.

"Who pissed off Elohim?" Zeke screamed above the din. He looked terrified. And I didn't blame him.

"You did!" I screeched back. "You did, you fool!" Looking around, I spotted Elliot hiding under a table, Billy running around like a chicken with its head cut off, and Eli cowering in the emptied pool.

Raising my face to the sky, I laughed gleefully, welcoming the rain, wind, and hail into my mouth, into my being. Feeling sweet release, I laughed hard and deep, uncontrollably, like a child giddy over a wish fulfilled on Christmas Day. Gagging and coughing after swallowing hunks of hail, I looked for a cup of water or soda. Nothing but broken glass, water-soaked plates of food, and assorted debris greeted my eyes.

And then, as quickly as it had started, it was over. Eerie silence hung in the air. After what seemed an eternity, we heard a voice. We all knew without question who was speaking. Elohim himself was addressing us four mortal peons. Fear paralyzed me. Was he coming for me? What fate did he have planned for us? Pain? Insanity? Hell? This was new territory. My fear had a new face. His name was Elohim.

The most powerful, awe-inspiring voice I could imagine boomed from the sky and reverberated throughout my trembling being: "Who dares to darken my counsel with words that have no knowledge?"

Nobody answered; nobody even moved.

Eli, who had sought refuge in the emptied pool, suddenly stood up and pointed. "There," he shouted, gesturing. He's over there!" He was indicating an unimposing figure we had assumed was a common pool bum who had been lounging on the other side of the cabana with a book across his face.

We had paid him no attention. But, in that moment, the unknown exploded into our world; it was Elohim!

"You asked me here, so here I am!"

I tried desperately to speak, but like a kid with his tongue stuck to a metal pole, all I could muster, was "Ehh, meh." I wanted to ask—no, I'm pretty sure we didn't—who is this? Is this Elohim? Is this a movie fantasy where everything gets switched around? The bum becomes king, the king is a peasant?

"Question for you, Job."

"Me?" I managed weakly, my voice faltering.

As if I'd never opened my mouth, he spoke words none of us would ever forget. "Where were you when I laid the earth's foundation? Just curious. Were you there when I marked off the dimensions of the deep, the firmament, the sky, the horizons? Have you ever spoken to the morning or showed the dawn its destination? Have you journeyed to the deepest springs of the sea or walked the recesses of the deep? Seen the gates of hell? What about Orion and the Bear? The infinite numbers of stars and constellations? Surely in your great wisdom, you can explain how thunderstorms, hail, wind, and rain work? By the way, did you like my demonstration?"

Never have I heard anything that so clearly emphasized the vast majesty and power of Elohim and my smallness and total inadequacy by comparison. Suddenly I understood: Who was I to question God's power, his wisdom, or his goodness? What injustice I had perpetrated by failing to trust him or his plan—no matter what hand life dealt me. As if someone had opened a fire hydrant and turned it on me full blast, his words overwhelmed me, making it hard to breathe.

Falling to my knees, I buried my head in my hands, ashamed. Awestruck by the demonstration of infinite wisdom and power, I quietly responded. "I know you can do all things. No plan of yours can be thwarted. Surely, I spoke of things I did not understand. Things too wonderful for me to comprehend." Hearing nothing, I continued. "My error was drawing conclusions on the basis of mere arrogance. Without seeing the deep things, the unknown things, I presumed in error."

Lost in the moment, my desire to justify myself disappeared; my arguments ceased to exist.

"I despise myself," I continued, broken. "No one else needs to take up my cause. I repent sincerely. Please . . . please forgive me."

There was no response, so slowly, I raised my head and looked around. Zeke's ugly mug grinned at me, his index finger slowly wagging, as if to say, I told you so.

But Elohim thundered, "Now, for the rest of you." Gesturing with his hand, he laid bare the group. What did he tell them? Well, that's between them and Elohim. Suffice it to say, Zeke blanched white and dropped his head like a guilty dog who'd been caught pooping on the floor. Elliot cringed in fright, like a child caught stealing a forbidden cookie. His eyes wide, Billy's head jerked like a rabbit caught in a snare, and Eli looked like he was going to throw up or pee his pants. Oddly feeling no joy in their discomfort nor moral superiority, I clamped my mouth shut and averted eye contact with anyone. Especially the speaker, as he continued.

"I'm angry with each of you. What you have said about Job is false. How convenient it is to have a scapegoat while you neglect dealing with your own pride and sin. Treat this man with respect. At least Job is authentic. You haven't been honest with me or about me."

Finally, he looked directly at me and addressed me once again: "Job, pray for your friends. Ask me to not treat them harshly for talking nonsense and for not being honest with themselves."

I did as I was told, and my friends were spared. Spared from what? Death? Funny, how quickly we forget that Elohim is the author *and* finisher of life. They begged for forgiveness and even brought me some sweet gifts to make up for my misery. After all, I no longer even had a cell phone!

In the blink of an eye, it was over.

My twins woke up in the hospital and asked for ice cream, my oldest son escaped his abductors, and my identity and good name were restored. Joy and I are still struggling to heal our marriage, but there is hope. There's always hope. Elohim is in control. Never doubt that; never despair; never waver.

ABADDON
June 24

Seething like a boiling cauldron, repressed like a coiled serpent, or exploding like an overheated canister, anger is my game. I play in anger like a grizzled old man weaving a tapestry of obscenities. The air turns blue, as I blend a mixture of semantics and linguistics to create vile, destructive threads of uncouth slang, cursing, and filth.

In my youth, I never knew when violence and rage would erupt from my subconscious. Then, as I supposedly grew wiser and more mature, I was expected to be tolerant and self-controlled, except for the occasional violent explosion of mind, mouth, and fists. But now, firmly established as the Prince of Darkness, there is no longer any reason for pretense of self-control. I act and behave as I feel. I push others to do the same. Watching Job and his friends angrily rip each other to shreds by the pool that day made for giddy entertainment.

But moments later, a different sort of rage inflamed my passion and threatened to blow through my eyeballs. When I realized that Elohim was there, I must admit, I completely lost my nerve. Just hearing his voice caused me to recoil in horror and quickened the beating of my heart. I gasped for breath through constricted air passages and my mind burned white hot with pain, blinding me to anything but him. My one thought was, Why do I hate him so much?

I wanted to enter the fray. In spite of my irrational blustering, I tried to think wisely. Should I risk it all and go for the jugular? Challenge Elohim once and for all to a fight to the finish? In spite of my boiling anger, fear started to overtake it. This was a battle I would not win today.

Not today. But mark my words: I *will* destroy mankind. One person at a time, each soul forever. Death is my canvas, and fear is my favorite color.

XVIII

Faith was the first seed to grow in Job's heart,
but repentance was the second.
Job's repentance was so complete that
Elohim canceled his guilt entirely.
Learn from Job. If you feel guilty,
repent and be made free.

JOB
June 25, 9:54 a.m. • *Lima Joe's Coffee Shop*

SLUMPED DOWN on a hard wooden chair, I shifted to find a more comfortable position. My eyes stared beyond the wood paneling ringing the wall of my favorite coffee shop. Had it all been just a dream? Funny how quickly we move on from strange memories. Like indigestion after a long-gone meal or the enjoyment of a particularly gripping episode of my favorite crime drama, it was now a fading memory.

But then it happened all over again. The coffee shop shifted. The walls folded, and suddenly I was back in the heavenly council. Upright and lucid, my eyes quickly adjusted to the brilliant light streaming from the sky. Floating like a hot-air balloon above the scene unfolding below me, I could hear, see, and feel that something amazing was about to transpire.

"Please stand and worship the God of all gods. The First, the Last, the Alpha, the Omega, the Beginning, the End. The great I Am! Worship Elohim!"

Praise erupted from the angelic hosts that crowded the heavenly council. Worship flowed from deepest passion. There was no pretense or spiritual arrogance, only pure, unfiltered, unadulterated love for Elohim.

The sound swelled as those in the sanctuary sensed his presence.

"Thank you for coming." Elohim's voice cut through the air, silencing all others. Every eye was focused on him; every ear strained to catch each word. "Thank you all for coming," he repeated, and then Elohim turned slightly sideways, tilted his head and pointed to Jesus. Thunderous applause resounded again through the tabernacle of the heavenly council, enveloping all in attendance.

After an entire minute of unchecked worship, Elohim held up his right hand. Instantly, the council grew silent.

"This is an important day," Elohim said solemnly. "Today, we will not be visited by unwanted guests; this is strictly for those whose hearts are in one accord with the Father, Son, and Spirit." The council erupted in applause. Elohim waited for it to subside before continuing. "I would like to begin by introducing you to my servant Job."

Reflexively, I sucked in my breath and held it. What? My name again? Why was this happening?

"Job, please come forward."

Surviving a tsunami of evil perpetrated by a crazed madman had been no easy feat, but Elohim was far more powerful than Abaddon. Had Elohim changed his mind about my pardon? Was I now about to die in the heavenly council? In a second, somber thoughts of doom flooded my mind as I considered various unpleasant methods Elohim could use to destroy me. A blazing sword of fire swirling through the air and plunging into my chest? A slinking serpent sinking its fangs into my shin? A simmering hole opening to rain-filled clouds as I'm hurled like debris into space?

A murmur of surprise was followed by puzzled silence in the chamber. This was clearly uncharted territory. Angels, cherubim, and seraphim uttered not even a single syllable. Bodies stilled lest a chair should squeak. Hands froze so not a paper would rustle nor the slightest sound escape. Breathing slowed to small, shallow swallows of air. Some turned blue, holding in coughs or sneezes. No one dared to break the silence as all waited to hear Elohim's next words.

"Job, you handled yourself with integrity and an amazing spirit of repentance," Elohim said, proudly. "Strong in the face of battle, you demonstrated unshakable faith and trust in me."

Unable to speak, I bowed my head and fell to my knees.

Suddenly, a powerful voice more regal than that of a king called out in triumph. Instantly, everything was changed. A low murmur grew until it had been transformed into throaty roars of approval.

"Yeshua is here!"

"The Son of God."

"Praise to the Father and Son."

Cheers rose in the throats of all in attendance as they recognized the voice of Yeshua:

"Salvation and power are established! The Accuser of our brothers and sisters has been thrown down to earth—the one who accuses them day and night before Elohim. They defeated him by the blood of the Lamb and by their testimony. They weren't in love with themselves. They were willing to die for Christ. Therefore, rejoice, O heaven!"

Spontaneous cries of praise and joy rose from the heavenly ranks as they celebrated every word from the Son of God.

"But terror is still to come on the earth and sea, for Abaddon has come down in wild and raging anger. His time is short, and he is acutely aware."

Without missing a beat, Elohim's voice rose in agreement:

"The Satan Project proves my diligence in keeping my word. If Job had been the only human who would suffer and refrain from evil and keep his faith, I still would have sent my Son. All of you are hereby commissioned to fight for my children. Encourage them to live in peace and to not be afraid. We hold the banner, we are the shield, even unto the end of time. Engage the enemy, slow his aggression, and silence his accusations."

Pausing, Elohim looked purposefully around the room, giving strength and hope to every creature, whether angelic or human.

"The Satan Project continues. His time is short."

• • •

JOB
June 26, 10:48 p.m. • 1457 Trillium Court

My eyes flicked open, and I reveled the comforting warmth
of my bed. Lying perfectly still to keep from disturbing my
wife, sleeping beside me, I let the events of the previous day
wash over my mind. Peace does not reign in every aspect of
my life. The residual damage lingers like stale bacon grease in
a forgotten skillet. Believing fables and lies, I had walked the
planet like an arrogant knight who had not yet tasted blood
in battle. Wielding pride like a shield, I had brandished confidence like a shameless social media hound. Today, beaten,
shamed, and humiliated, my pride stripped painfully away,
I no longer walk in naiveté. Abaddon, seeking to devour
all who enter his domain, has trained his sights squarely
upon the frail, weak children of Elohim. Picking them off
one by one, he continues his quest to murder every human
ever born.

My body and mind are now primed for battle. From now
on, as I walk through life, my right hand will remain out-
stretched to help fellow pilgrims in need, but my left will
tightly hold the sword of the Spirit—the Word of God—
with which I'll strike if provoked, fight if attacked.

My fight is not a solitary one; Elohim, Jesus Christ, Topek,
and many others have formed a garrison to surround me. We
fight together. My adversary has been named, but it's my
King who reigns.

Closing my eyes, I pull the covers tight and roll onto my side. In spite of the darkness around me, I smile. I am not afraid. Elohim is with me in the dark.

Where once was darkness, now hope shines.
Where once was hate, now love springs.
Where tears once fell, now joy flows.
Where friendship once died, loyalty grows.
Where lies were once spoken, truth now shouts.
When last breath fades, life remains.
When lost and alone, home beckons.

—Job